# About Reading Connection:

**W**elcome to RBP Books' Connection series. Reading Connection provides students focused practice to help reinforce and develop reading skills in areas appropriate for sixth-grade students. Reading Connection uses a variety of writing types and exercises to help build comprehension, thinking, phonics, vocabulary, language, reasoning, and other skills important to both reading and critical thinking. In accordance with NCTE (National Council of Teachers of English) standards, reading material and exercises are grade-level appropriate. Clear examples and instructions on each page guide the lesson. Activities help students develop reading skills and give special attention to vocabulary development.

Dear Parents and Educators,

Thank you for choosing this Rainbow Bridge Publishing educational product to help teach your children and students. We take great pride and pleasure in becoming involved with your educational experience. Some people say that math will always be math and reading will always be reading, but we do not share that opinion. Reading, math, spelling, writing, geography, science, history, and all other subjects will always provide some of life's most fulfilling adventures and should be taught with passion both at home and in the classroom. Because of this, we at Rainbow Bridge Publishing associate the greatness of learning with every product we create.

It is our mission to provide materials that not only explain, but also amaze; not only review, but also encourage; not only guide, but also lead. Every product contains clear, concise instructions, appropriate sample work, and engaging, grade-appropriate content created by classroom teachers and writers. The material is based on national standards to support your best educational efforts. We hope you enjoy our company's products as you embark on your adventure. Thank you for bringing us along.

Sincerely,

George Starks
Associate Publisher
Rainbow Bridge Publishing

# Reading Connection™ • Grade 6
## Written by Greg Larson

Illustrations
Jonathan Hallett

Visual Design and Layout
Andy Carlson, Robyn Funk, Zachary Johnson, Scott Whimpey

Publisher
Scott G. Van Leeuwen

Editorial Director
Paul Rawlins

Associate Publisher
George Starks

Copy Editors and Proofreaders
Patricia Harvey, Linda Swain

Series Creator
Michele Van Leeuwen

Technology Integration
James Morris, Dante J. Orazzi

Please visit our website at
**www.summerbridgeactivities.com**
for supplements, additions, and corrections to this book.

First Edition 2003

For orders call 1-800-598-1441
Discounts available for quantity orders

ISBN: 1-932210-21-0

PRINTED IN THE UNITED STATES OF AMERICA
10 9 8 7 6 5 4 3 2 1

# Table of Contents

# 6th Grade Suggested Reading List

**Alexander, Lloyd**
Book of Three
High King
Drackenberg Adventure

**Alphin, Elaine Marie**
The Ghost Cadet

**Armstrong, William H.**
Sounder

**Banks, Lynne Reid**
The Indian in the Cupboard
The Return of the Indian
The Secret of the Indian

**Biesty, Stephen**
Stephen Biesty's Incredible
Cross-Sections

**Billingsley, Franny**
Well Wished

**Byars, Betsy**
After the Goat Man
Pinballs
Cracker Jackson
Cybil War
The Midnight Fox

**Cooper, Susan**
The Grey King
Silver on the Tree

**Coville, Bruce**
Jeremy Thatcher, Dragon
Hatcher
The Skull of Truth

**Creech, Sharon**
Absolutely Normal Chaos

**Dahl, Roald**
Matilda

**Fleischman, Sid**
The 13th Floor: A Ghost Story

**Franklin, Kristine L.**
Lone Wolf

**George, Jean Craighead**
The Fire Bug Connection
Julie of the Wolves
My Side of the Mountain
On the Far Side of the Mountain

**Greer, Gery**
This Island Isn't Big Enough for
the Four of Us

**Ibbotson, Eva; illustrated by
Kevin Hawkes**
Island of the Aunts

**Jacques, Brian**
Redwall

**Jennings, Paul**
Uncovered!: Weird, Weird Stories

**Konigsburg, E.L.**
From the Mixed Up Files of Mrs.
Basil E. Frankweiler

**Lewis, C.S.**
The Magician's Nephew
Prince Caspian

**Le Guin, Ursula K.**
The Farthest Shore

**Lowry, Lois**
The Giver

**McKay, Hilary**
The Amber Cat

**McKinley, Robin**
The Blue Sword

**Naylor, Phyllis Reynolds**
All But Alice
The Bodies in the Besseledorf
Hotel
The Fear Place

**O'Brien, Robert C.**
Mrs. Frisby and the Rats of NIMH

**O'Dell, Scott**
Sing Down the Moon
The Black Pearl

**Patterson, Katherine**
Bridge to Terabithia
Great Gilly Hopkins

**Paulsen, Gary**
Brian's Winter

**Peck, Robert Newton**
Soup's Goat

**Rappaport, Doreen**
Escape from Slavery: Five
Journeys to Freedom

**Roberts, Willo Davis**
View from the Cherry Tree
Who Invited the Undertaker

**Rocklin, Joanne**
For Your Eyes Only!

**Rodowsky, Colby F.**
Clay

**Ruckman, Ivy**
No Way Out

**Sachar, Louis**
Holes
There's a Boy in the Girls'
Bathroom

**Seidler, Tor**
Mean Margaret

**Snyder, Zilpha Keatley**
Velvet Room

**Soto, Gary**
Baseball in April and Other
Stories

**Speare, Elizabeth George**
Sign of the Beaver
The Witch of Blackbird Pond

**Spinelli, Jerry**
The Library Card
Wringer

**Taylor, Theodore**
Timothy of the Cay

**Wardlaw, Lee**
101 Ways to Bug Your Parents

**White, Ruth**
Belle Prater's Boy

**Voight, Cynthia**
Homecoming

**Yep, Laurence**
Dragongate

**Zindel, Paul**
The Pigman and Me

# The Assignment

How will Ben win the respect of his new teacher and classmates?

"All right, then," Mr. Brakey said as he stood in front of the class. He cleared his throat as if to speak more clearly, but it was more of a subtle message for the students to be quiet and listen.

Ben's desk was on the front row. He turned around to see who was still talking. He glanced at different students, trying to put names with faces. His family had moved into the area only two weeks ago, so he was the new kid in class and was still trying to find friends.

Most of the kids were turning their attention to the front and waiting patiently. A pencil poked into Ben's back, and he whipped around in his seat to face Gary. Gary pointed at Mr. Brakey, and Ben turned back to see Mr. Brakey looking down at him very seriously.

"All right, then," Mr. Brakey repeated. "Your writing assignment for this unit is to write a story about your ancestors who immigrated to this country. This can't be just one or two paragraphs. This has to bring together your personal family history with what we've been studying about immigration. So talk to your parents or other relatives, and then make a captivating short story out of your research."

That night at dinner, Ben explained the assignment to his parents, and they talked about their ancestors. He remembered some of the stories he had heard before. One ancestor had been a drummer boy in the American Revolution. One couple had run away from Ireland because her father had forbidden them to marry. Other ancestors had come from Italy, Denmark, Germany, and Spain. They all had their own struggles and their own stories.

Ben went to his room after dinner and sat down to write a story. He was determined to write the best story he had ever written. It would be so good that Mr. Brakey would stand up in front of the class and say, "I want to read this remarkable short story to you." Ben could envision himself being complimented by some of the students, and he could see new respect for him in their eyes.

Ben stared blankly at the paper, wishing the story would come to him. But it wouldn't come, and he grew more and more frustrated. Maybe it would be easier to write it on the computer, he thought. But he stared at the blank page on the screen, and his fingers didn't move on the keys for what seemed like an hour.

Finally he decided he needed a break, so he put on a game. He became Aragorn, swinging his sword in battle with fierce orcs. The battle intensified. His fingers and thumbs flashed on the controls, and then suddenly they weren't keys, but the cold steel of a sword handle in his hands, and he wasn't staring at a screen, but into the ugly face of an angry, evil orc.

www.summerbridgeactivities.com  Reading Connection—Grade 6—RBP0210

## Expanding Your Reading Power

1. Check the word or phrase that describes Ben in the story.
   _____ part of the "in" crowd
   _____ lazy
   _____ goal setter

2. Check the word or phrase that best describes Ben's motivation.
   _____ Ben wants to get out of work.
   _____ Ben wants to win the respect of the teacher and other students.
   _____ Ben wants to have a girlfriend.

3. What do you think will most likely happen next?
   _____ Ben finds himself in a fantasy world.
   _____ Ben gives up on his writing project.
   _____ Ben gets back at Gary for poking him.

## Expanding Your Word Power

Write the words from this story that have the meanings below.

1. not obvious _____

2. people you have descended from _____

3. moving from one country to another _____

4. fascinating _____

5. to picture in one's mind _____

6. became more forceful _____

7. Check the sentence in which *kid* has the same meaning as in paragraph two.
   _____ The nanny goat was nursing her kid.
   _____ She warned the boys to not kid about the problem.
   _____ Nixon had been president when his mother was a kid.

8. Check the sentence in which *whipped* has the same meaning as in paragraph three.
   _____ Alex whipped around the corner.
   _____ He wanted whipped cream on his pie.
   _____ The Roman soldier got whipped as his punishment.

## Understanding Language

A **suffix** is a letter or group of letters added to the end of a word to change the word's meaning or part of speech. The suffix **-ly** usually means "in a certain way." Find the words from the story that have the suffix **-ly** added to these base words; then write those words in the blanks.

1. clear _____

2. patient _____

3. serious _____

4. blank _____

5. sudden _____

## Expanding Other Skills

Below is a map outlining the countries of Europe. Use an atlas, encyclopedia, or the Internet to locate the countries of Ben's ancestors. Write the letter of the country next to its name.

1. Ireland _____

2. Italy _____

3. Denmark _____

4. Germany _____

5. Spain _____

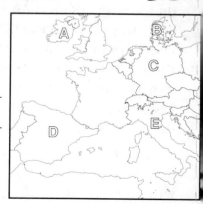

Ben had no time to think about what had just happened to him, and he stared in disbelief. The disagreeable orc bared his rotting teeth and raised his club, ready to smash Ben. Never in his life had Ben held a real sword in his hands, but in his imagination he had been a sword-wielding hero in stories he had read, in movies he had watched, and especially in the hours of video games he played.

As the orc brought down the club, Ben jumped to the side and brought the sword into position to swing. But the orc reacted quickly, raising the club to parry the sword stroke.

Back and forth Ben and the orc swung the sword and the club, just as Ben had done so many times before when it had only been a game. But now he felt himself sweating and his muscles straining. He felt the rocks under his feet. His hands hurt each time the sword and club smashed together. And his nose was filled with an awful stench that could only have been orc odor.

Around they went, circling each other in a peculiar dance, swinging their weapons and parrying the blows. Then the orc blocked Ben's path. Ben glanced over his shoulder and saw his disadvantage. They were approaching the edge of a cliff. If the orc could not crush him with his club, he would push him off the cliff!

Ben saw the orc's move as he started to charge. Ben dove at the orc's feet, just as he had once dived in desperation at the feet of a running back on the opposing football team as he dashed down the sideline. The orc tripped over Ben and fell face first onto the rocks at the cliff's edge, but his momentum pulled him forward and he slid, grabbing at the loose rocks before he disappeared over the edge.

Ben lay on the ground, sucking in air to catch his breath. He closed his eyes and then opened them wide, hoping this was only a bad dream and that he could wake himself from it. But he was still on the rocks. His hands and arms hurt, and the gleaming sword was by his side.

After resting, he got up and found the place where he had first come face to face with the orc. He looked around but had no idea how he had come to this place or how he would get out. There seemed to be a trail, so he followed it a short way until he saw a campfire and, near the campfire, a girl bound by a tree. He approached, distrustful, looking for more orcs, but there were none. Ben used the sword to cut the girl free from her bindings and removed the gag in her mouth.

"Thank you, Ben," she said. "I've been waiting for you."

www.summerbridgeactivities.com   Reading Connection—Grade 6—RBP0210

## Expanding Your Reading Power

1. Check the word that best describes the mood of this story.
   _____ tense
   _____ relaxed
   _____ humorous
   _____ pleasant

2. Write the word that best completes this sentence.
   Ben's agility was helped by his participation in _____.
   **chess club         reading         football**

3. Check the reason Ben was able to fight with a sword.
   _____ He had taken fencing lessons.
   _____ He had practiced virtual sword fighting (in video games).
   _____ He was just good at sword fighting, like his parents.
   _____ He was just lucky.

4. Check the word that most closely describes the setting of this story.
   _____ fantasy
   _____ space travel
   _____ real life
   _____ true history

## Expanding Your Word Power

Write the words from this story that have the meanings below.

1. showed _____
2. to deflect or ward off _____
3. bad odor _____
4. unusual or odd _____
5. recklessness arising from despair

   _____
6. continuing motion_____
7. shining_____

A **metaphor** is a figure of speech in which two objects or ideas are compared directly, without using *like* or *as*.

8. Check the correct meaning of the metaphor *in a peculiar dance* from paragraph 4.
   _____ They were dancing to music.
   _____ They were moving around each other.

9. Check the correct meaning of the metaphor *to catch his breath* in paragraph 6.
   _____ He was trying to stop breathing so hard and fast.
   _____ He was trying to capture the air from his lungs.

## Understanding Language

A **prefix** is a letter or group of letters added to the beginning of a word to change the word's meaning. The prefix **dis-** means "not" or "opposite of." Write the words from the story that have the prefix **dis-** added to these base words.

1. belief _____
2. agreeable _____
3. advantage _____
4. appear _____
5. trust _____

## Expanding Other Skills

Dictionaries organize word entries in alphabetical order. Write the following words in alphabetical order.

| | |
|---|---|
| agile | _____ |
| momentum | _____ |
| campfire | _____ |
| cautious | _____ |
| bare | _____ |
| parry | _____ |

"Who are you, and how do you know my name?" Ben asked.

The girl with the strange glow, or the enchanted creature, or whatever she was, smiled at Ben. He had just rescued her, but her smile reassured him, telling Ben that she was going to help him.

"My name is Clio," she replied, and although she was only talking, her voice lilted like soft music. "And I know much more about you than just your name, but right now you are full of many questions that need answers. 'What is this place?' 'How did I get here?' 'Why am I here?' 'How can I get back to where I came from?'"

Ben nodded, but before he could speak, Clio reached out her delicate hand toward him. "Come with me, Ben, and you'll start to get your answers. Leave the sword here. You won't need it."

Ben dropped the sword and took her hand lightly in his own. As he did, a jolt of strange energy flowed through him. Slowly they lifted off the ground. Then the ground seemed to retreat beneath them, and almost instantly they landed on top of a high mountain in the warm glow of the sun.

"Behold Fabulaterra!" Clio said.

Ben gazed in wonder at the world below. If this was a

dream, it was the best dream he had ever had, and he was not eager to wake up. But it was too real to be just a dream.

"Look!" Clio said, pointing in the direction of a scene coming into focus. It was like a movie, except it was not on a screen. It seemed to be real life happening right in front of him.

Ben saw himself at different homes in which he had lived. His family had moved often, and in each new place, before he had made friends, he had spent a lot of time by himself. He read stories and novels or created his own comic books, either in traditional style or in Japanese animé style.

"Only those with a powerful imagination enter Fabulaterra," said Clio, "and only after they have struggled do they get this far."

The scene in front of Ben evolved, and he saw himself trying to write the story for Mr. Brakey's class. It had been a struggle because he wanted his story to be as good as any of the stories written by his favorite authors.

"Most people only come as far as the gates of Fabulaterra, where they are entertained by the parade of spectacles that come out," Clio said. "But from here, inside Fabulaterra, you will learn answers to questions you didn't even know to ask."

www.summerbridgeactivities.com
Reading Connection—Grade 6—RBP0210

## Expanding Your Reading Power

1. Authors write stories for many reasons. Check the most likely reason the author had for writing this story.
   _____ to inform
   _____ to entertain
   _____ to persuade

2. Check the word or phrase that best describes Clio in this story.
   _____ harsh
   _____ caring
   _____ selfish

3. Check the sentence that best states the main idea of this story.
   _____ A person can go many places in his or her imagination.
   _____ It's not good to move too often.
   _____ A person cannot learn how to write stories.

4. Check what will most likely happen next.
   _____ Clio will disappear.
   _____ Ben will wake up from a dream.
   _____ Clio will help Ben learn to use his imagination in his writing.

## Expanding Your Word Power

Write the words from this story that have the meanings below.

1. restored confidence in _____
2. spoke musically _____
3. small or easily damaged _____
4. a sudden shock _____
5. impatient with desire _____
6. developed or achieved gradually _____
7. public performances or displays _____

A **simile** is a figure of speech in which two unlike things are compared using *like* or *as*.

Write the actual meaning of these similes.

8. Her voice lilted like soft music.

   _____

9. It was like a movie, except it was not on a screen.

   _____

## Understanding Language

The prefix **re-** means "back" or "again." Write the words from the story that have the prefix **re-** and are formed using these base words.

1. assure _____
2. treat _____

Write the words from the story that have the suffix **-ly** and the following meanings.

3. in a light way _____
4. in a slow way _____
5. in an instant way _____

## Expanding Other Skills

**Guide words** are the two dark words at the top of a dictionary page. These words help you find words in the dictionary more quickly. Write the words from the box that would be on the page with the guide word pairs listed below.

| aura   enchant   evolve   animé |
|---|

1. Europe—example _____
2. angle—answer _____
3. empty—ensemble _____
4. auction—automatic _____

# J. R. R. Tolkien

How did he learn to write such imaginative stories?

"The boy you see had a powerful imagination like you do," said Clio. "Observe."

Ben watched. He saw a priest conducting a funeral for a young father. A young mother cried into her handkerchief. Four-year-old Ronald sat on one side of his mother, and his younger brother, Hilary, sat on the other side.

Ronald's father had been working in a bank in South Africa. After he died, Ronald's mother moved the family back to England. They settled in Birmingham, not far from Wales. As young Ronald was learning to read English, he was intrigued by how different the Welsh names were that he saw on coal trucks coming from and going back to Wales—names like "Penrhiwceiber," "Senghenydd," and "Nantyglo." Young John Ronald Reuel Tolkien was falling in love with language.

Then another tragedy struck. When Ronald was only 12, his mother died of diabetes. The parish priest took over the responsibility for Ronald and Hilary. He saw their intelligence and made sure they received the best education possible. Ronald had a special aptitude for language. He learned Latin and Greek and then went on to Gothic and Finnish. For fun, he used the power of his imagination to invent his own languages. And he started writing stories.

He met other boys who were interested in literature and writing. They met after school for snacks and to share their writing. They called their club the Tea Club Barrovian Society, or T.C.B.S., since they always met for tea (an afternoon English snack or meal) at the Barrow's Store.

The close friendship continued as the boys became men. When World War One broke out, each of them enlisted in the army. Tolkien was a second lieutenant and went to the front lines in the trenches. War had been portrayed as noble, but Tolkien found the reality of war to be ugly. All the members of the T.C.B.S. were killed in the war except Tolkien and one other friend. This caused Tolkien to reflect more deeply than ever before on the good and evil in the world. After four months, Tolkien became deathly ill with "trench fever" and was transferred back to England, where he spent the rest of the war.

Tolkien became a professor at Oxford University. Together with his good friend C. S. Lewis, he helped form another club for writers called the Inklings.

One night as he was grading papers, he absent-mindedly wrote on a blank sheet, "In a hole in the ground there lived a Hobbit." He had no idea what a hobbit was, but he decided to let his imagination find out. So he wrote stories about hobbits for his children.

"Ben," Clio said, "the ugly, evil orc you fought came out of the imagination of J.R.R. Tolkien, the same imagination that first created the good and likable hobbits."

www.summerbridgeactivities.com

## Expanding Your Reading Power

1. Check the word or phrase that best describes Tolkien when he comes home from the war.
   _____ eager to get back to the front lines
   _____ upset about the evils of war
   _____ lazy

2. A **fact** is something known to be true. An **opinion** is what people believe, but it may or may not be true. Write **F** for each fact and **O** for each opinion.
   _____ Diabetes can cause death.
   _____ Learning languages is fun.
   _____ War is noble.
   _____ Hobbits are imaginary creatures.

3. Number the events to show the order in which they happened.
   _____ Tolkien fights in World War One.
   _____ Tolkien's father dies.
   _____ Tolkien creates hobbits in stories.
   _____ The Tolkiens' move back to England.

4. A **summary** is a brief statement of the most important details. To summarize, decide which details are most important, and then put them in an order that makes sense. In one sentence, summarize the information in paragraph six.

   _____

   _____

## Expanding Your Word Power

Write the words from this story that have the meanings below.

1. having curiosity aroused _____
2. a natural talent or inclination _____
3. signed up to join the armed forces _____
4. described or represented _____
5. moved from one place to another _____
6. without thinking _____

**Synonyms** are words that have the same or similar meanings. Write the words from this story that are synonyms for these words.

7. force _____
8. brilliance _____
9. create _____

**Abbreviations** are short forms of words or groups of words. Write the words from the story that are represented by these abbreviations.

10. Eng. _____
11. T.C.B.S. _____
12. WWI _____

## Understanding Language

A **base word** can stand alone as a complete word, or it can take prefixes or suffixes. **Word roots**, however, cannot stand alone. They are always combined with other word parts to make words. The word root -**duc**- or -**duct**- means "lead" or "direct." Find the words from the story with the word parts listed below added to the root -**duc**- or -**duct**- and write the words.

1. con- _____ -ing (paragraph 2)
2. e- _____ -ation (paragraph 4)

## Expanding Other Skills

Below is a map of western England and eastern Wales. It includes lines for longitude (distance to the east or west) and latitude (distance to the north or south).

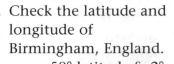

1. Check the latitude and longitude of Birmingham, England.
   _____ 50° latitude & 2° longitude
   _____ 52°, 30 min. latitude & 2° longitude
   _____ 51°, 30 min. latitude & 20° longitude

2. Check the direction you would travel from Birmingham, England, to Nantyglo, Wales.
   _____ southwest          _____ west
   _____ northwest          _____ south

# The Hobbit
What is a hobbit anyway?

Ben had been entranced by the movies of the Lord of the Rings trilogy, and the video games based on the movies were his favorites.

"Children born through one imagination survive in the imaginations of others," Clio said. "Meet one of those children."

"Hello, my boy," said a voice behind Ben.

Startled, Ben turned quickly to see who had spoken. He looked down on a person about three feet tall with a happy, good-natured face beneath a heavy mop of curly, brown hair. The little person wore bright green pants and a bright yellow shirt under a green vest but had no shoes on his hair-covered feet.

"Bilbo Baggins," said the little person, extending his hand.

"I'm Ben." As they shook hands, Ben noticed that Bilbo's brown fingers were much longer than his own, and the phrase "clever fingers" popped into his mind.

"You want to know about the adventures Mr. Tolkien put me in, me and the dwarves and Gandalf the Gray, when he was still a gray wizard. Of course, Mr. Tolkien used Gandalf to get me involved, when I would much rather have stayed home in the Shire in Bag-End, my comfortable hobbit hole—hobbit holes have round doors and round windows, you know, with all the comforts anyone could want. You'll have to come visit some-time, and we'll have a splendid meal together."

Bilbo Baggins spoke quick-ly, without giving Ben a chance to respond.

"Anyway, Ben, those 13 dwarves wanted to get back their treasure deep inside Lonely Mountain, treasure that had been stolen by a dragon called Smaug, and they wanted me, a respectable hobbit, to sneak in and steal the treasure. Now hobbits are not thieves, but we can walk without making noise, and we can see in darkness better than most creatures. So we started out…"

As Bilbo told his story, the scenes opened up in front of Ben. He saw the group of adventur-ers captured and almost eaten by trolls. He saw them visiting the elves at Rivendale, fighting with orcs and wolf-like wargs, and being saved by eagles. He saw Bilbo finding a magic ring that made the wearer invisible and winning a contest of wits with Gollum, the night creature who wanted to eat Bilbo. He saw them fighting giant spiders and escaping in barrels down a river.

"In Lonely Mountain, there was a hobbit-sized hole and a tunnel to Smaug's lair. I used the ring of invisibility and more than usual hobbit care to make no sound. Past the sleeping drag-on I crept. I took a two-hand-ed cup, and made it back to the dwarves. But then Smaug awoke and knew a piece of his treasure was missing! Such fury and fire!

"But, alas, now it's my time for tea. Let's meet again soon, and I'll tell you the rest of the story. Good day."

And with that, Bilbo Baggins disappeared.

## Expanding Your Reading Power

1. Check the most likely reason the author had for writing this story.
   _____ To describe a hobbit.
   _____ To make people write fantasy fiction.
   _____ To introduce readers to Tolkien's book *The Hobbit*.

2. Write **H** before statements that describe hobbits, **HB** before statements that describe human beings, and **H & H** before statements that describe both.
   _____ They are about three feet tall.
   _____ They live in your neighborhood.
   _____ They never wear shoes.
   _____ They like to live in comfortable homes.

3. Check the most likely conclusion to Bilbo Baggins's adventure in *The Hobbit*.
   _____ The dwarves never get their treasure.
   _____ Bilbo returns home after a successful adventure.
   _____ Smaug kills all the members of Bilbo's group.
   _____ The dragon takes back his cup.

## Expanding Your Word Power

Write the words from this story that have the meanings below.

1. fascinated _____

2. a group of three books on a related subject
   _____
   _____

3. surprised; frightened _____

4. enlarging; putting forth _____

5. included; drawn into _____

6. worthy; proper in conduct _____

7. den or dwelling of a wild animal _____

**Antonyms** are words that have opposite meanings. Write the words from this story that are antonyms to these words.

8. die _____

9. slowly _____

10. light _____

## Understanding Language

A **compound word** is formed by putting two or more words together to make a new word. Some **compound words** are two words with a **hyphen** between them. Write the hyphenated compound words from this story containing these base words.

1. nature _____

2. hair _____

3. hand _____

## Expanding Other Skills

An **outline** is a way of grouping information and showing how information is related. Complete this partial outline of paragraphs 7 through 11 of this story.

**I.** Bilbo Baggins
   **A.** Where Bilbo lived
      **1.** name of the area: _____
      **2.** name of his hobbit hole (house):
         _____
   **B.** Bilbo's adventure with the dwarves and Gandalf
      **1.** captured by _____
      **2.** visiting _____ in _____
      **3.** fighting with _____ and _____
      **4.** being saved by _____
      **5.** finding a magic _____
      **6.** in a contest of wits with _____
      **7.** fighting giant _____
      **8.** escaping on a river in a _____
      **9.** sneaking into the lair of _____

"I could never be a writer like Tolkien," Ben said.

"No, but you can be a writer like Ben," Clio answered. "Tolkien had a fertile imagination, and he nourished it on stories and legends. That's why you are here in Fabulaterra, to nourish your imagination and help you learn the language of stories. We'll start with some of the legends that inspired Tolkien."

A new scene appeared before Ben. He saw an elderly fisherman and his wife on a bleak island under a leaden sky.

"The fisherman calls himself Grimner, but he is in disguise," Clio said. "He is actually Odin, father of the gods. Odin and his wife, Frigga, have crossed the rainbow bridge from Asgard, city of the gods, to Midgard, the world of men and women. They have been searching for those who have the strength and spirit to be heroes and save the world from the power of the malicious giants. They saw that Agnar and Geirrod, sons of King Hrauding, have this potential, so they have arranged to teach them."

Ben saw young Agnar and Geirrod fishing on the ocean from a dinghy. A sudden squall drove the boat to the island and smashed it on the rocks. Odin saved the boys and took them to his hut.

"Now we shall see which boy can become the noblest hero," whispered Odin to Frigga that night. Frigga favored Agnar, the elder brother, who was kind and observant and spoke with a gentle voice. Odin favored Geirrod, who was passionate and brash and spoke with a boisterous voice.

Through the winter, Odin taught the boys how to hunt bears and catch great fish. He had them challenge their bravery by climbing rocky cliffs and jumping across wide and deep chasms. Each performed well, but Geirrod always pushed himself to outshine Agnar.

Sometimes, however, while Frigga spun her wool, Agnar stayed by her side listening carefully to her stories of the struggle between the gods of Asgard and the giants of Jötunheim. His wisdom grew as Frigga answered his probing questions, and Frigga came to know of Agnar's determination to help the gods of Asgard fight the evil of the giants.

In the spring they finished a boat Odin had been helping the brothers build. "Someday, I will visit you," said Odin. "Remember that even a king should show hospitality to a poor fisherman."

Agnar rowed most of the way home. Then Geirrod told Agnar to rest while he rowed. When Agnar was asleep and land close by, Geirrod turned the boat around and threw the oars overboard. "You shall never claim your birthright as king," Geirrod whispered, and he slipped into the sea and swam to land as the boat drifted back to the deep ocean.

## Expanding Your Reading Power

1.  List three things Odin and Frigga did to train the boys to be heroes.

    a. _____

    b. _____

    c. _____

2.  Check the word that best describes Agnar in this story.

    _____ sad

    _____ compassionate

    _____ competitive

3.  Check the word that best describes Geirrod in this story.

    _____ quick

    _____ compassionate

    _____ competitive

4.  Check all of the likely outcomes of this story.

    _____ Agnar will be lost at sea.

    _____ Geirrod will go back to help his brother.

    _____ Geirrod will become king.

    _____ Odin will try to visit the boys.

## Expanding Your Word Power

Write the words from this story that have the meanings below.

1.  highly productive; capable of creating _____

2.  sustain; provide what is needed for growth _____

3.  barren; gloomy _____

4.  dull, dark, and gray _____

5.  small rowboat _____

6.  alert; quick to perceive _____

7.  hasty and unthinking _____

8.  noisy and unrestrained _____

9.  a deep crack in the earth gorge _____

10. deep-searching investigation _____

In each row below, circle the two words that are related to the word in bold type.

11. **writer**    author    novelist    golfer

12. **hut**    garden    shack    shanty

13. **stories**    tales    problems    dramas

## Understanding Language

Write the compound words from the story that are formed by adding to these base words.

1.  fish _____

2.  rain _____

3.  birth _____

## Expanding Other Skills

Study this temperature table for Sweden and then answer the questions below.

| Average Daily Temperature in Celsius for Stockholm, Sweden | | | | | | |
|---|---|---|---|---|---|---|
| | November | December | January | February | March | April |
| High | 5 | 2 | -1 | -1 | 3 | 8 |
| Low | 1 | -2 | -5 | -5 | -4 | 1 |

1.  What temperature is the freezing point on the Celsius scale?

    _____

2.  During which months might you expect to find ice in the sea off the coast of northern Sweden?

    _____

3.  If Odin's island had been in the sea off Sweden, during which month after winter ended could Agnar and Geirrod have left the island in a boat?

    _____

Odin returned to Asgard still concerned about what might happen in the world. He had two ravens, Hugin and Munin, to help him keep track of events. Each day they left Asgard and flew throughout all the worlds and then returned to tell Odin all that they had seen and heard.

One day Odin went to the top of the watchtower and waited for them, but they did not return. The next day, they flew back to Odin and landed on his shoulders. He took them into the Council Hall and sat on his throne as they told him of forebodings of evil.

Odin did not tell the other gods of his apprehensions, but Frigga read them in his eyes. "You must visit the Norns," she said. "Then you can know which way the wind blows and whether these forebodings are valid."

Odin crossed a rainbow bridge to Yggdrasil, the tree of life. At the base of the tree was Urda's well, the Well of Fate. Three sisters sat by the water. Urda, the eldest sister, was goddess of the past. Verdandi, the middle sister and the most beautiful, was goddess of the present. Skulda, the youngest, was goddess of the future, and she kept her face hidden by pulling her hair over it. But Odin saw through Skulda's hair and read in her eyes her sorrow for the future.

When Frigga saw Odin's eyes, she knew his forebodings had been verified. "I must go to Mimir's Well where I can add wisdom to this knowledge." Odin told her. "There is much work to be done

with mankind, and I will need wisdom to help change things for the best."

So Odin left Frigga and the gods and goddesses of Asgard. He left his golden armor, his eagle helmet, and his magic spear that never missed its mark. Wearing a dark blue cloak and hat and carrying a traveler's staff, he became Vegtam the Wanderer. He traveled through Midgard to the border of Jötunheim, the land of the evil giants. There he came to the Well of Wisdom.

"Hail, Odin," said Mimir, overseer of the well. Mimir drank daily from the well and was not fooled by Odin's disguise.

"I have need to drink from the Well of Wisdom," said Odin.

"Yes, I know," replied Mimir. "Many come to drink, but no one has been willing to pay my price. Will you pay my price, king of the gods?"

"I will," said Odin, "for I need wisdom to help mankind."

Then Mimir dipped his horn into the water, and Odin drank. Immediately his eyes were opened to understanding and his mind to wisdom.

"The price is your right eye," said Mimir.

Without hesitation, Odin plucked out his right eye and handed it to Mimir, who dropped it into the water. There it remained as a sign of the price the father of the gods paid for his wisdom.

## Expanding Your Reading Power

1. Check the word that best describes Odin in this story.

_____ brave

_____ foolish

_____ concerned

_____ selfish

2. Write **T** before statements that are true. Write **F** before statements that are false.

_____ Hugin and Munin were Odin's goats.

_____ *Verdandi* was the tree of life.

_____ Odin wanted to be wise so he could help mankind.

_____ Mimir was the overseer of the Well of Wisdom.

3. Write the word that best completes this sentence.

A person who believes in _____ believes the future can't be changed.

**legends**       **wisdom**       **fate**

4. Check the sentence that best states the main idea of this story.

_____ There is no such thing as magic.

_____ Knowledge and wisdom are extremely valuable.

_____ Birds make good pets.

_____ Rainbows are bridges between heaven and earth.

## Expanding Your Word Power

Write the words from this story that have the meanings below.

1. hints of future misfortune _____

2. uneasy feelings about the future_____

3. having the truth or accuracy proven _____

4. supervisor or director_____

5. slowness to act or decide _____

6. pulled off or out of _____

An **idiom** is a phrase that cannot be understood by the meaning of its words alone. The phrase "burn the midnight oil" is an idiom. It means to work or study late into the night.

7. Find the idiom in paragraph 3 of this story and write it here.

_____

## Understanding Language

The suffixes **-sion** and **-tion** mean "have the condition of" or "being in the state of." Write the words from the story that combine the suffix **-sion** or **-tion** with these base words.

1. apprehend_____

2. hesitate _____

Write the words from the story that combine the suffix **-ly** with these base words.

3. final _____

4. immediate_____

## Expanding Other Skills

Traveling in Odin's day was very different from traveling today. Today you can go all over the world and find the same signs to help find things. Match the service with the correct sign.

1. _____ hospital      **a.**

2. _____ restaurant      **b.**

3. _____ airplane      **c.**

4. _____ showers      **d.**

5. _____ parking      **e.**

6. _____ information      **f.**

# Seeking Geirrod and Agnar

What has happened to the two sons of King Hraulding?                    Odin's Heroes, part 3

Odin, disguised as Vegtam the Wanderer, walked through Midgard to the land of King Hrauding. He was the king whose young sons, Geirrod and Agnar, Odin had once trained to become heroes. As Odin approached the house of the king, a group of men on dark horses rode up furiously from behind him, almost knocking him to the ground as they passed. They reined in their horses in front of the stable and shouted for servants to take their horses. Only one servant came out of the stable to take the horse of the leader. The other men called harshly to the Wanderer to take their horses and, laughing gruffly, they strode to the king's house.

"Is this not the house of King Hraulding? And who are these uncouth men?" Odin asked the servant, though Odin knew the answer.

"Good King Hrauding has died, and his son Geirrod now rules."

"But what of Agnar, the son of the birthright?"

"He was lost, and his whereabouts are not known," said the servant, bowing his head. But the disguise of the servant did not fool Odin. Geirrod did not know that Agnar had returned and was disguised as the servant, but Odin knew full well.

After they cared for the horses, Agnar gave bread to the stranger and invited him to stay for the night. Odin thanked Agnar, but said that he would rely on the hospitality of the king for a dinner of meat and a warm place to stay.

"Better to stay here and sleep on the straw," Agnar warned, "for the king is in his usual foul mood, and you will not be received well."

Odin thanked Agnar again, then departed for the main house, where he knocked on the door and asked the porter for warmth, food, and rest in the king's hall.

"Not in this king's hall!" the porter snarled, blocking the Wanderer's way.

"Let him in, and we'll have our fun," shouted one of the men.

When Odin stood before Geirrod and his men, he knew that the brave boy for whom he had such high hopes had instead become a selfish despot and a leader of thieves.

"Sing to us while we eat, old man," said Geirrod, "and if your song pleases us, you shall have some leftover meat."

The Wanderer stood between two pillars and sang about an ambitious young prince who, having forsaken any good within him, had become evil and had gathered followers who were criminals. As Odin sang, Geirrod gradually realized that this Wanderer was condemning him with his song.

"Seize him!" Geirrod ordered his men, and they bound Odin to the pillars with chains.

"You came for warmth, and warmth you shall have," Geirrod growled as his men piled wood around the stranger and set it ablaze.

## Expanding Your Reading Power

1. Check the word that best describes the mood of this story.
   _____ tense
   _____ humorous
   _____ pleasant

2. List two facts that lead you to conclude that King Geirrod is a criminal.
   a. _____
   b. _____

3. Do you think King Geirrod and his men will kill Odin? Why or why not?
   _____
   _____
   _____

4. Check all the ways this story shows the reader what King Geirrod is like.
   _____ what Geirrod does
   _____ what Geirrod says
   _____ what Geirrod thinks
   _____ what other characters say about him

## Expanding Your Word Power

Write the words from this story that have the meanings below.

1. fiercely _____
2. held back _____
3. harshly _____
4. crude and unrefined _____
5. tyrant _____
6. a strong desire to achieve _____

Write the words from the story that are synonyms (words that have the same or similar meanings) for these words.

7. prepared _____
8. reigns _____
9. deceive _____
10. heat _____

## Understanding Language

A **possessive** is a word that shows ownership or relationship. The singular possessive is usually formed by adding 's to a word, such as "king's hall." Rewrite each phrase below. Use possessives.

1. house of King Hrauding
   _____

2. disguise of the servant
   _____

3. hospitality of the king
   _____

Write the compound words from the story that are formed by adding to these words.

4. where _____
5. left _____

## Expanding Other Skills

Here is a recipe that could have been used when the myths about Odin were being told.

Recipe for
Norwegian Sanbakkel Cookies

| | |
|---|---|
| 1 egg | ½ c almonds, ground |
| 1 c sugar | 2 ½ c flour |
| 1 c butter | |

Beat egg. Add sugar, butter, and almonds. Mix well. Add flour. Mix thoroughly and roll very thin. Cut with cookie cutter. Bake in 375° F oven for 10 to 15 minutes.

1. What is the relationship between the order of the ingredients and the directions?
   _____
   _____

2. What other information might you want to know about this recipe?
   _____

# Rewarding Geirrod and Agnar
How will Odin reward the two brothers?

Odin's Heroes, part 4

The fire burned hot and furious, but the Wanderer was not consumed. Geirrod and his men marveled and left the stranger chained between the pillars.

King Geirrod ordered his servants to give no food or drink to the stranger in chains. However, after Geirrod and his men departed the next day to find people to rob and houses to plunder, Agnar brought food and drink to Odin.

That night, Geirrod and his men returned from their robbery, ate like wolves at the table, and again set fire to wood under the stranger. Again, after the fire died, the stranger stood unscathed, and Geirrod and his men wondered.

For seven more days, Geirrod and his men left to rob and plunder, and Agnar gave food and drink to Odin. And each night, Geirrod had his men try to burn the stranger.

On the ninth night, Odin sang again, his voice filling the hall and beyond. He sang how the gods had prepared Geirrod to become a noble hero, but instead he had chosen to become like a wild beast. The vengeance of the gods, he sang, was about to fall on evil King Geirrod!

"Come closer, Geirrod, and see Grimner the fisherman who gave you hospitality and affection and who trained you to be good, as well as strong and brave. Come closer and see that Grimner was in truth Odin, who stands before you now and who will reward you with what your evil deeds deserve!"

As the song ended and the flames died, the chains fell from Odin. Furious, Geirrod rushed at Odin with his sword, but with each blow, Odin remained unharmed. Then Odin grabbed the sword from Geirrod.

Geirrod backed away in terror from the terrible gaze in Odin's eyes. Geirrod's men shrank back with their king, and as they huddled in the corner, Odin changed them into a pack of wolves.

"You chose to be beasts, and beasts you shall be!" Odin yelled as he chased them from the house. "Deep in the dark forest you shall live, and there you shall wander forever!"

The servants and other subjects of King Geirrod who heard the commotion crowded into the king's hall, cheering now that they were freed from King Geirrod and his henchmen.

Odin handed the king's sword to the stable servant. "People of good King Hrauding, behold your new king, King Agnar, rightful heir to the throne! Not only is he kind and wise, but you shall also see that he will be stronger and more victorious than his brother, all for the good of mankind and the purposes of the gods."

And it was so.

## Expanding Your Reading Power

1. Write **G** before statements that describe Geirrod, **A** before statements that describe Agnar, and **GA** before statements that describe both.

   _____ He was a prince, the son of a king.
   _____ He was kind and giving.
   _____ He was mean and selfish.
   _____ He was a successful king.

2. Which sentence best states the main idea of this story?

   _____ It's important to give hospitality to guests.
   _____ Elected leaders are better than kings.
   _____ Criminals will pay for their crimes.

3. Number the events in the order they happened.

   _____ Geirrod abandons Agnar and swims to shore.
   _____ Agnar works as a stable servant.
   _____ Geirrod tries to kill Odin.
   _____ King Hrauding dies.
   _____ Geirrod becomes king.
   _____ Odin seeks hospitality from King Geirrod.
   _____ Agnar becomes king.
   _____ Odin turns Geirrod and his men into wolves.

4. Write a short summary of what happened to Agnar after he returned from the sea.

   _____

## Expanding Your Word Power

Write the words from this story that have the meanings below.

1. eaten up _____
2. to rob by force _____
3. unharmed _____
4. welcoming guests _____
5. violent action _____

6. loyal followers in bad actions _____
7. person entitled to inherit _____
8. Find the simile in paragraph 3 and write it.

   _____

9. Explain what the simile actually means.

   _____

   _____

## Understanding Language

The prefix **un-** means "not" or "opposite of." Write the words from the story that combine the prefix **un-** and these base words.

1. scathe _____
2. harm _____

The suffix **-ous** means "characterized by." Write the words from the story that combine the suffix **-ous** and these base words.

3. fury _____
4. victory _____

## Expanding Other Skills

Write the name of the best reference to use to find the information below.

| atlas | almanac | dictionary |
| encyclopedia | | a book of myths |

1. definition of the word *henchmen* _____
2. a map of Scandinavia _____
3. more stories about Odin _____
4. histories of Scandinavian countries _____
5. facts about climates in Scandinavia _____

Odin was concerned about the threat of evil becoming more powerful in the world. He used his powers to help men and women grow into heroes and heroines who would fight for good. Heroes needed strength, courage, and skill for battle. He had helped Agnar and Geirrod develop those qualities. But he saw that true heroes and heroines also needed wisdom, integrity, and compassion. Agnar had developed those qualities, but Geirrod had not.

With the other gods, Odin created Kvasir, a man of unsurpassed knowledge and wisdom. Kvasir was a poet whose words made people love and remember the wisdom he taught them. Kvasir traveled throughout Midgard reciting his profound poetry and teaching wisdom. Odin was pleased that men and women were gaining wisdom, integrity, and compassion.

One day Odin's ravens, Hugin and Munin, returned from flying through the worlds to report that Kvasir was missing. He had last been seen going with some dwarves into their mountain.

Odin left Asgard and crossed the rainbow bridge to Mimir's Well.

"I sense that evil is at work to prevent mankind from gaining wisdom," Odin said to Mimir.

"Indeed," replied Mimir. "Gaze into the water of the well, and you shall see

what has happened to your poet and messenger of wisdom."

The water stirred into small ripples, then calmed as clear as glass. Odin saw Kvasir coming upon a group of dwarves near their mountain home. When they discovered he was the poet Kvasir, they invited him for a banquet in his honor. Deep into the mountain they traveled.

The band of dwarves prepared an elaborate meal and then invited Kvasir to recite his poetry and teach them wisdom. Never before had these dwarves heard such elevating poetry. Never before had they been so excited by the ideas of goodness and kindness.

However, Fialar and Galar, the leaders of the band, were distraught. They had not been with the band when Kvasir had been invited into the mountain. They did not want to accept the ideas of goodness and kindness that would turn their band away from mischief. But when they argued with Kvasir, his wisdom showed the falseness of their logic.

Kvasir was slain that night as he slept. Wisdom and poetry ran through Kvasir's veins. Fialar and Galar captured this wisdom and used it to brew the Magic Mead of Wisdom and Poetry. Then they sealed the mead into three pots, where it would grow stronger.

## Expanding Your Reading Power

1. Write **F** for each statement of fact and **O** for each statement of opinion.

   _____ Kvasir was the greatest poet.

   _____ The dwarves' meal was delicious.

   _____ Odin tried to help mankind.

   _____ Fialar and Galar killed Kvasir.

2. Check the statement that best describes the main idea of this story.

   _____ Wisdom is a valuable treasure.

   _____ Dwarves are cruel.

   _____ Wisdom is not for everyone.

3. Number the events in the order they happened.

   _____ The dwarves brew a magic mead of wisdom.

   _____ Odin and the gods create a poet of great wisdom.

   _____ Kvasir is invited to a banquet with the dwarves.

   _____ Kvasir is slain.

## Expanding Your Word Power

Write the words from this story that have the meanings below.

1. high moral values _____

2. caring _____

3. not topped _____

4. deep and meaningful _____

5. detailed or complicated _____

6. raising _____

7. extremely upset _____

8. Find the simile in paragraph 7 and write it.

   _____

   _____

9. Explain what the simile means.

   _____

   _____

## Understanding Language

The suffix **-ness** means "condition" or "quality." Write the words from the story that have the suffix **-ness** and the meanings below.

1. quality of being good _____

2. quality of being kind _____

3. quality of being false _____

## Expanding Other Skills

Here is another recipe that could have been used for banquets in Scandinavia.

Match the abbreviation with the appropriate word.

Honey Mead

4 lb. raisins
1 med. lemon
1 tsp. grated nutmeg
1 qt. honey
6 med. cinnamon sticks
2 ½ gal. soft rainwater
1 clove
½ c rosewater

1. _____ cup            **a.** med.

2. _____ teaspoon       **b.** qt.

3. _____ quart          **c.** lb.

4. _____ gallon         **d.** c.

5. _____ medium         **e.** tsp.

6. _____ pound          **f.** gal.

7. Which three ingredients are spices?

   _____

   _____

   _____

# Dwarves and Giants

What will the dwarves do with their magic mead?                Odin and the Magic Mead, part 2

"Once we drink in the power of words from the magic mead," said Fialar, the dwarf, "we can do anything we want and talk our way out of the consequences!"

Galar laughed gleefully at the thought of the terrible mischief they could get away with. "Why wait? Let's start now," he said. "How about Gilling, the giant who gave us such insult?"

Neither Fialar nor Galar could remember exactly what Gilling had done to insult them long ago; nevertheless, they plotted for revenge. They invited Gilling to a feast by the sea. They fed him, then took him for a ride in a boat. When they were far out to sea, Gilling stretched out and went to sleep. Once he began to snore, the dwarves capsized the boat, and they all tumbled into the ocean. Then, while Gilling splashed and shouted for help, Fialar and Galar righted the boat and rowed back to shore.

The dwarves got others in their band to join them as they traveled about Jötunheim, finding more ways to make mayhem and torment the giants. They grew bold, making up songs boasting of their evil deeds.

Suttung, the son of Gilling, was a powerful and cunning giant. Through the dwarves'

songs he learned what had happened to his father. Suttung tracked down the dwarves, and at night, while they were sleeping, he scooped them up into a whale net. He carried them into the sea near where his father had fallen from the boat and placed them on a large rock that was gradually being covered by the incoming tide.

"You shall soon know how my father felt to be alone against the sea," Suttung told them.

The terrified dwarves wailed and cried for mercy. "Take us out of this ocean, and we will give you gold and jewels!"

Suttung laughed. "I don't want your gold and jewels."

"Save us, and we will give you the Magic Mead of Wisdom and Poetry!" Fialar cried.

Suttung took the dwarves off the rock, but kept Fialar and Galar in the net while the others went to fetch the magic mead from their caverns. When he had the magic mead, Suttung released the dwarves.

"Now man shall not have this wisdom from the gods, and the war shall be won by the giants!" Suttung said to himself as he strode toward home.

## Expanding Your Reading Power

1. How did Suttung find out what had happened to his father?

   _____

   _____

   _____

   _____

2. Write **D** before the statements that describe dwarves, **G** before the statements that describe giants, and **DG** before statements that describe both.

   _____ They wanted the power of the magic mead.

   _____ They were larger than human beings.

   _____ They were smaller than human beings.

   _____ They lived inside a mountain.

Write the word that best completes this sentence.

3. Losing respect is a natural _____ of boasting.

   **consequence    accusation    insolence**

## Expanding Your Word Power

Write the words from this story that have the meanings below.

1. results_____

2. joyfully _____

3. turned upside down_____

4. stone used to grind grain _____

5. torture _____

6. cried in high-pitched voices _____

7. caves_____

Write the words from this story that have the meanings below.

8. starved _____

9. awake _____

10. dropped_____

11. emptied _____

## Understanding Language

If a plural word ends in *s*, the possessive of that word is formed by adding only an apostrophe after the *s* (**s'**). For example, the plural possessive of *student* is *students'*. Write a sentence that includes the plural possessive form of each of these words.

1. giant_____

   _____

2. husband_____

   _____

3. song _____

   _____

4. son _____

   _____

## Expanding Other Skills

Some Important Water Safety Rules

Complete the rules by adding the appropriate phrases.

| flotation devices    a buddy |
| :---: |
| the shallow end    gum or food |

1. Swim with _____.

2. If you are learning to swim, stay in

   _____.

3. Check_____to make sure they are Coast Guard approved.

4. Don't chew _____while you swim—you could choke.

# Odin in the Land of the Giants

Odin gazed into the water of Mimir's Well and saw the giant Suttung carrying the Magic Mead of Wisdom and Poetry to his home. Suttung put the three pots of mead in his treasure chamber inside a mountain. Since the mead was more valuable than any gold, jewels, or other treasure, he put his daughter, Gunnlod, inside the chamber to guard it. Then he built a thick rock wall across the entrance. Gunnlod was a beautiful maiden, but to make her a better guard, her father enchanted her, turning her into a frightful witch with long teeth and sharp nails. She was so ugly all she wanted was to hide in the chamber.

Odin disguised himself as the Wanderer and started walking for the home of Suttung. As he got close, he passed a wheat field belonging to Baugi, brother of Suttung. Nine men with scythes were struggling to cut the grain.

"Let me sharpen your scythe for you," said the Wanderer to one of the men.

The Wanderer took a whetstone from his belt and with a few strokes quickly sharpened the blade. All the men were amazed at the ease with which this scythe now cut the grain.

"Sell us your whetstone," they all begged, "for it must be magic!"

"Whoever would want it may have it for the cost of a meal," the Wanderer said as he tossed the whetstone into the middle of the group. As an argument arose over the ownership of the whetstone, the Wanderer left for Baugi's home.

Baugi received the Wanderer with gracious hospitality, and soon they were eating a fine meal at a great table. But the meal was interrupted when a distraught serving maid burst into the room.

"Master Baugi, it is a tragedy! Your nine serfs in the field got into an argument over the whetstone, and now there is no one left to harvest the wheat!"

Baugi jumped up from the table and paced. "What can I do? We cannot get through the winter unless my grain is cut, and I have no other workingmen!"

"I shall work for you," said the Wanderer, "and I shall do the work of nine men. Tomorrow you shall see."

Baugi did not believe it could be, but the next day, the Wanderer worked in Baugi's field and indeed did more work than nine serfs. That night at supper, Baugi begged the Wanderer to stay until the entire field was cut and the work of the season completed. Baugi promised the Wanderer any reward if he would stay.

When the Wanderer completed all the work of the harvest, he went to Baugi to claim his reward. "All I ask," he said, "is a drink of your brother's magic mead."

"I don't know if I can get that for you," Baugi said. Then he looked past the Wanderer to his full barns and said, "But a bargain is a bargain, and I will do whatever I can."

© RBP Books          www.summerbridgeactivities.com          Reading Connection—Grade 6—RBP0210

## Expanding Your Reading Power

1. How did Suttung feel about his daughter?
   _____ He loved his daughter more than his treasure.
   _____ He loved his treasure more than his daughter.
   _____ He wanted her to be happy.
   _____ He was proud of her.

2. Write two of the ways Odin showed his magic powers.
   a. _____
   _____
   b. _____
   _____

3. Do you think Suttung will give the magic mead to Baugi for Odin? Explain.
   _____
   _____
   _____

## Expanding Your Word Power

Write the words from this story that have the meanings below.

1. having high value_____

2. put under a spell_____

3. scary_____

4. a tool with a long, curved blade for cutting _____

5. a stone for sharpening blades _____

6. generous, courteous _____

7. Check the sentence in which *hide* has the same meaning as in paragraph 1.
   _____ The leather in her belt was made from the hide of a buffalo
   _____ Where will you hide your Easter eggs?

8. Check the sentence in which *grain* has the same meaning as in paragraph 2.
   _____ It is easier to cut wood with the grain than across the grain.
   _____ His favorite sandwich was made with seven-grain bread.

9. Check the sentence in which *season* has the same meaning as in paragraph 11.
   _____ Winter can be a harsh, long season in Alaska.
   _____ The cook used pepper and paprika to season his stew.

## Understanding Language

Rewrite the phrases below using possessive forms.

1. land of the giants _____

2. water of Mimir's Well _____
   _____

3. home of Suttung_____

4. work of nine men_____
   _____

5. work of the season _____
   _____

## Expanding Other Skills

Dictionaries often divide entry words into **syllables**. A syllable shows where words can be divided at the end of a line of writing. Write the words below and place dashes between the syllables.

1. valuable _____

2. ownership_____

3. hospitality_____

4. wanderer _____

Reading Connection—Grade 6—RBP0210          www.summerbridgeactivities.com          ©RBP Books

Baugi went to his brother, Suttung, and explained about the man who saved him by doing the work of nine men and then asked for a drink of the magic mead as his reward.

"Brother, you are a fool!" cried Suttung angrily. "Who among men could do the work of nine men? What if this Wanderer is one of the gods? That is why I have enchanted my daughter, Gunnlod, and locked her away in my treasure chamber to guard the mead—so that no god or man shall have any of it! Should any men drink of it, their words of wisdom should spread. They would side with the gods, and our power with men will diminish!"

Baugi returned to his guest with the bad news and asked the Wanderer to claim a different reward. "That is the only payment I will take," said the Wanderer, "and I hold you to your bargain. If your brother will not give it willingly, we must get it some other way. Lead me to Suttung's treasure chamber."

Baugi led the Wanderer to the mountain cavern. The entrance was blocked with a thick wall of stone that neither of them could budge.

"If I could help you, I would," said Baugi, "but you see, it is impossible."

The Wanderer took a long auger from inside his cloak and handed it to the giant. "You have the strength, giant. Bore me a hole through this rock wall."

The giant worked the auger with all his strength and bored a hole that finally penetrated the wall.

"Thank you," said the Wanderer, and suddenly he turned into a snake and crawled into the hole. When Baugi saw this he knew the Wanderer was one of the gods who had tricked him to get to the magic mead. He stabbed at the snake with the auger, but it was too late.

Inside the treasure chamber, Odin changed into his normal form, which to Gunnlod looked like a handsome young giant.

"Don't look at me!" she screeched, putting up her gnarled hands to block his view.

Gently Odin took her hands in his. "Gunnlod, you were once beautiful, and you can be again. Trust me to bring that beauty out again."

Odin kissed her hands. Gunnlod felt her fingers soften. Odin looked deep into her eyes and then kissed her lips. Gunnlod felt the red blood of youth return to her cheeks. For three days Odin stayed with Gunnlod and reversed the enchantment. In the end, Gunnlod was even more beautiful than before.

Gunnlod willingly surrendered the Magic Mead of Poetry and Wisdom to Odin and showed him the secret passage out of the mountain. Odin returned to Asgard with the magic mead, which he would carefully dispense to worthy men and women. And Gunnlod, who had tasted of the mead, wandered through the worlds, singing of the goodness of Odin and of her love for him.

## Expanding Your Reading Power

1. Check the most likely reason the author had for writing this story.
   _____ to persuade
   _____ to entertain
   _____ to give directions

2. Check the two words that best describe Gunnlod before she meets Odin.
   _____ confident
   _____ ashamed
   _____ hopeless
   _____ happy

3. Write the word that best completes this sentence.
   Spending your money will _____ your savings.
   **penetrate**        **reverse**        **diminish**

4. Number the events to show the order in which they happened.
   ____ Odin goes to the land of the giants.
   ____ Suttung refuses to give any magic mead to the Wanderer.
   ____ Odin earns a reward from Baugi.
   ____ Odin makes Gunnlod beautiful again.
   ____ Baugi drills a hole into Suttung's treasure chamber.
   ____ Odin obtains the magic mead for mankind.

## Expanding Your Word Power

Write the words from this story that have the meanings below.

1. to make less _____
2. a tool for boring _____
3. to make a hole _____
4. went through _____
5. twisted, misshapen _____
6. turned back _____
7. distribute _____

In each row below, circle the two words that are related to the word in bold type.

8. **chamber**    book        vault        room
9. **cloak**      cape        coat        timepiece

## Understanding Language

The prefix **im-** means "not." Write the meaning of each of these words.

1. impolite _____
2. impossible _____
3. impatient _____
4. immobile _____
5. immovable _____
6. impure _____

## Expanding Other Skills

The graph shows the diameter of holes bored for different purposes. Under each bar on the graph, write the letter of the item matching the size of the hole.

**a.** electrical power cord    =    25 mm
**b.** fence post             =    70 mm
**c.** sewer line             =    230 mm
**d.** fence post             =    150 mm

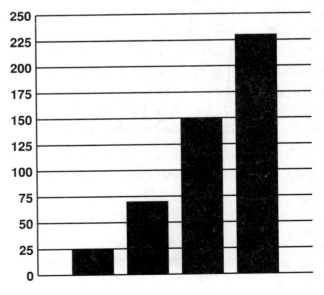

# Thor's Hammer Disappears

Why is a hammer so valuable?                                    Thor's Hammer, part 1

Odin had many sons who helped him protect men and the gods. Odin's son Thor was more famous among men and more feared among giants than any of his brothers. Tall and powerfully built, Thor had a shaggy, flaming red beard and hair and fiery red eyes that flashed like lightning when he was angry.

Thor's main weapon was a massive, magic hammer named Miolnir, the Crusher. Miolnir was so heavy that in order to wield it, even huge Thor needed a magic belt that doubled his own remarkable strength. Miolnir was so hot and so fiery, that Thor also needed a magic iron glove to hold it.

Heimdall, the god who guarded the rainbow bridge that connected Asgard to the other worlds, would not allow Thor and Miolnir to use the bridge. The gods were concerned that all that weight could break the bridge or that all that heat could melt it. So Thor always traveled through the clouds. When he was angry, Thor threw Miolnir. In Midgard men and women saw the trail of fire when the hammer was thrown, and they called it lightning. They heard the booming crash of Miolnir and called it thunder. Part of the magic of the hammer was that it always returned to Thor when he threw it.

There was nothing the giants of Jötunheim feared more than Thor and Miolnir. The gods made Thor vow to never let Miolnir out of his sight, for Thor was the main protector of Asgard.

However, one morning when Thor woke, he reached for Miolnir and it was gone! Quickly, he searched the area, but it was nowhere. "Awwwwwww!" he yelled, his voice shaking Asgard.

At first he suspected Loki, a god who was always playing tricks. With his fiery eyes blazing, Thor grabbed Loki by the throat. But this time Loki was innocent and even promised to help Thor find the magic hammer.

Loki took Thor to elegant Freya, the most beautiful of the goddesses and queen of the Valkyries.

"Would you lend me your white feather cape?" Loki asked. "I must fly to the other worlds to search for Thor's hammer."

Freya knew Asgard was in danger if Thor didn't have his hammer, so she willingly lent her priceless magic cape. Loki put on the cape, and with a flash of light, he turned into a white raven.

Loki flew straight to Jötunheim, land of the giants, for they had the most to gain by depriving Thor of Miolnir. He flew high above Jötunheim searching for Thrym, the king of the giants, who was cunning and malicious enough to have captured Thor's hammer.

© RBP Books        www.summerbridgeactivities.com        Reading Connection—Grade 6—RBP0210

## Expanding Your Reading Power

1. Why would the giants want Thor to lose his hammer?

   _____

2. Check the word that best describes Thor.
   _____ pleasant
   _____ shy
   _____ wimpy
   _____ mighty

3. Write **F** for each statement of fact and **O** for each statement of opinion.
   _____ Thor was scary.
   _____ Thor was Odin's son.
   _____ The weight of Thor and his hammer would break the rainbow bridge.
   _____ Freya was a goddess and a queen.

4. Check the most likely next development of this story.
   _____ Loki really did take the hammer.
   _____ The giants capture Loki.
   _____ Loki, the white raven, is attacked by an eagle.
   _____ Loki discovers that the giants stole the hammer.

## Expanding Your Word Power

Write the words from this story that have the meanings below.

1. bulky, large _____
2. promise _____
3. suspended loosely _____
4. tasteful and refined _____
5. invaluable _____
6. taking away _____
7. skilled at deceiving, shrewd _____
8. with a desire to harm _____

Write the words from the story that are synonyms (words that have the same or similar meanings) for these words.

9. guard _____
10. joined _____
11. pranks _____

## Understanding Language

The word root **-mal-** means "bad." Write the word from the last paragraph of the story with this meaning.

1. characterized by being bad _____

Write the meaning of the following word.

2. malnutrition _____

Rewrite the phrases below as **possessives**.

3. magic of the hammer

   _____

4. booming crash of Miolnir

   _____

5. protector of Asgard

   _____

6. queen of the Valkyries

   _____

## Expanding Other Skills

Complete this partial outline from this story.

I. Magic items

   A. Thor's magic items

      1. _____

      2. _____

      3. _____

   B. Freya's magic item

      1. _____

Loki, in the form of a white raven, flew toward the palace of Thrym, king of the giants. He finally spied the king on top of a hill, grooming a herd of horses surrounding his knees.

"What have you done with Thor's hammer?" Loki asked, flying high above the giant's reach.

Thrym laughed so hard, boulders fell from the nearby mountain. "I know you, Loki," he roared, "and it's true! I have Thor's thunder hammer, and it's buried eight leagues beneath the frost. You will never find it, and Thor shall never have it again!"

"The gods will recompense you for the hammer," said Loki. "Think of our treasure—do you not covet Odin's ring, or the necklace of Brising? Name your price."

"I have treasure, and with Thor's hammer gone, my giants can go to Asgard and take all your treasures," said Thrym. "The only treasure I would barter for Miolnir is Freya willingly giving herself to me as my bride!"

Loki flew back to Thor and Freya and explained Thrym's demand.

"I absolutely refuse!" shouted Freya. "I could never give myself to that witless, ugly giant, even for Miolnir!" Thor begged her, but she would not relent.

The gods called a council. Without Thor's hammer to protect them, all of their attention and energy would be needed to protect Asgard, and they would never again be able to help mankind.

But they could not bring themselves to force beautiful Freya to marry Thrym and live in Jötunheim. All seemed hopeless.

Then Loki stepped forward and said, "Let us pretend to give Freya to Thrym. One of the gods will go in disguise wearing a bridal dress and veil, and he will demand Miolnir before the marriage."

"But which god should go?" they asked.

"He who lost the hammer," Loki replied.

All eyes turned to mountainous Thor, and each god worked mightily to stifle his laughter at the ridiculous image of Thor in a wedding gown with a garland of flowers on his head.

"Never!" roared Thor.

"My son," said Odin, "you are the only one who can control Miolnir."

Thor hesitated and then, pointing his finger at the council, roared, "If I do, you must all swear that none of you will laugh at me for this!"

"We will swear," said Odin. "And Loki, you will go with Thor dressed as his bridesmaid."

The bride and bridesmaid's gowns were sewn and fitted. The gods and goddesses dressed Thor in a white gown with red embroidery, a sash of housekeeper's keys hanging at his side, and in a veil thick enough to cover his bristly red hair and beard. A garland of flowers rested on top of his head. Freya put her bridal jewels around his neck and across his chest. Loki also wore a dress and veil. They were ready for their journey to Jötunheim, land of the giants.

## Expanding Your Reading Power

1. Check the word that best describes the mood of this story.

    _____ tense

    _____ relaxed

    _____ humorous

    _____ pleasant

2. Write **F** for each statement of fact and **O** for each statement of opinion.

    _____ Thrym was taller than a horse.

    _____ Thor was the greatest of the gods.

    _____ Thor was a beautiful bride.

    _____ The gods wanted to be able to help mankind.

3. Check the most likely conclusion about Loki.

    _____ He is always trusted.

    _____ He never gets in trouble.

    _____ He is good at fooling others.

4. What will most likely happen next in this story?

    _____ The giants are not fooled by the disguises.

    _____ Thor and Loki never make it to the land of the giants.

    _____ The giants invade Asgard.

    _____ Thor gets his hammer back.

## Expanding Your Word Power

Write the words from this story that have the meanings below.

1. cleaning and brushing_____

2. about three miles each _____

3. reward or pay for _____

4. crave or desire _____

5. trade _____

6. soften one's resolve _____

7. hold back or suppress _____

8. fabric decorated with needlework

    _____

Write the words from the story that are **antonyms** (words that have the opposite meaning) of these words.

9. distant _____

10. thin_____

## Understanding Language

The suffix **-less** means "not having" or "without." Write the words from the story with the suffix **-less** and these base words.

1. wit_____

2. hope _____

Write the meaning of each word below.

3. helpless _____

4. doubtless_____

5. motionless _____

## Expanding Other Skills

1. You could use different reference sources to find information about historical bridal gowns. Write 1 before the best source and 2 before the second-best source.

    _____ almanac

    _____ newspaper

    _____ atlas

    _____ encyclopedia

    _____ internet

    _____ book about historical costumes

2. If you wanted to learn about sewing, what are two good reference sources you could use?

    a. _____

    b. _____

# The Wedding

Can Thor and Loki fool the giants?                              Thor's Hammer, part 3

The gods sent a messenger ahead of the bride and bridesmaid so that Thrym could prepare the wedding feast. As the bride and bridesmaid approached, Thrym rushed out to meet them.

"Welcome, beautiful Freya, whom so many giants have sought to win, and who will now be mine alone!"

Thor remained silent. Thrym turned to the bridesmaid. "Why does she not speak?" he asked suspiciously.

"When she heard she was to marry the great king Thrym, she shouted for joy these eight days, and now she is hoarse," Loki said.

"Oh, yes, I understand," said the conceited giant.

When they sat down for the feast, the giants were amazed to watch the bride ravenously devour eight large salmon. Loki kicked Thor under the table, but Thor paid no attention and went on to eat a whole ox.

This time the bridesmaid leaned over to Thrym and said, "Poor thing, she has been so anxious about meeting you and getting married that she has not eaten one bit in the eight days we have been traveling."

"Poor, sweet darling," said the giant king. "She is nervous to marry the great king of Jötunheim!"

With that, Thrym lifted the corner of the veil to kiss his bride, but when he saw two fiery eyes he quickly dropped the veil and jumped back. "Why are her eyes so red?" Thrym asked the bridesmaid.

"It is the fire of love," Loki responded.

"Then she should wait no longer!" Thrym roared. "Let us marry this bride to her hero!"

"But first we need Thor's hammer!" Loki said.

King Thrym gave the command. It took four giants to carry in the hammer and place it in front of the bride.

"Let the stupid oaf Thor have back his hammer," said Thrym. "I shall possess the most beautiful goddess now and still possess Asgard another day!"

Thor's heart leapt when he saw Miolnir. He grabbed the hammer, threw back the veil, stood up, and shouted, "I am not Freya, but Thor! Taste of my vengeance!"

Thrym drew his sword, but Thor was quicker, and he struck the giant to the ground, yelling, "There is your wedding present, Thrym!"

The other giants grabbed weapons and rushed at the gods, but Thor and Loki, still dressed in wedding garments, defeated them all.

Thor and Loki rushed outside, and with one powerful blow from Miolnir, the great hall of Thrym crashed to the ground.

There was great feasting at Asgard when the two gods returned. Thor laughed uproariously as he and Loki told the details of their adventure, and Thor released the others from their vow so that they might laugh with him.

## Expanding Your Reading Power

**1.** Check the word or phrase that best describes Thrym.

_____ generous

_____ kind

_____ self-centered

**2.** Check the main conflict in this story.

_____ person vs. person

_____ person vs. nature

_____ person vs. society

_____ person vs. himself (internal conflict)

**3.** Number the events in the order they happened.

_____ Thor disguises himself as the bride, Freya.

_____ Thor's hammer is stolen.

_____ Loki makes excuses for the bride's strange behavior.

_____ Thor uses his hammer to destroy the giants.

_____ Loki learns who took the hammer.

_____ Thrym gives Thor's hammer to the bride.

_____ Thrym promises to return the hammer if Freya will marry him.

**4.** Write a short summary about the qualities of Thor's hammer.

_____

_____

_____

_____

## Expanding Your Word Power

Write the words from this story that have the meanings below.

**1.** low, husky sounding _____

**2.** vain_____

**3.** in a hungry way _____

**4.** eat up greedily_____

**5.** clumsy person _____

**6.** clothes _____

**7.** loudly_____

**Homophones** are words that have the same sound but different spellings and meanings. Write the **homophones** of the following words from the story.

**8.** a head _____

**9.** hoarse _____

**10.** pore/pour _____

## Understanding Language

Write the words from the story with the suffix **-ous** or **-ously** that have these meanings.

**1.** with suspicion _____

**2.** in the manner of a raven; predatory; extremely hungry_____

**3.** with noisy excitement_____

## Expanding Other Skills

A **pronunciation key** shows sound symbols and key words to explain how to pronounce dictionary entry words. Use the pronunciation key in your dictionary to understand the sound of the words below; then write the regular spelling.

**1.** sôt _____

**2.** hôrs_____

**3.** fir' _____

**4.** ôf_____

# The Wrong Hunger

What value would you place on wisdom?

Laughter rang from the halls of Odin's palace as Thor and Loki told their story. At times the noise of the laughter and its echoes were so loud it almost hurt Ben's ears, but he laughed as if he were sitting right in the middle of the feast, and he wiped his mouth because the aroma of the food made him salivate. Then the scene faded, and the great Viking hall with all its feasters and revelers vanished. Ben's laughter subsided, but his stomach still growled with hunger.

Ben realized then that he was still on top of a high mountain, sitting in a patch of soft grass in the warmth of the sun. What had Clio called this place? Fabulaterra, or something like that. Whether this was a dream or not, he was liking it a lot. But still, it wasn't home, and he couldn't just go to the refrigerator to get some leftover pizza and juice. Or if not pizza and juice, then chocolate chip cookies and cold milk would taste great right now.

He looked around for Clio and saw her sitting on top of a giant mushroom, her legs crossed, her chin in her hand as she studied him. "That was awesome!" Ben said. "Totally amazing! But can I go home now?"

Clio didn't answer right away, and Ben felt uncomfortable, as if she were looking inside of his mind. Then she said quietly, "Ben, you're listening to the wrong kind of hunger."

At first Ben thought that maybe his stomach was growling, but then he realized she meant something else. "What do you mean?" he asked.

"Why did Odin go to Mimir's Well? Was he thirsty for water?"

"No, what he really wanted was wisdom," Ben answered.

"How much was he willing to give in exchange for wisdom?"

"He would give almost anything," Ben said. "He felt that getting wisdom was more important than keeping one of his eyes."

"How about you, Ben? How hungry are you to gain wisdom and understanding?"

"Okay, you're right. Missing a snack or even skipping a meal wouldn't be too much to sacrifice to learn something important."

Clio smiled and said, "Ben, you have real potential to achieve big things. I can tell, and I have chosen to help you as I helped Tolkien and others you will meet."

"But when can I go home?"

"When you can give me the right answer to one question: What is the purpose of stories?"

Ben didn't take long to think before he said, "They're fun."

Clio slid down from the giant mushroom. "When you know their real purpose, you'll start to understand why most of them are so fun or rewarding." She reached out her hands, directing a new scene to open. "You're going to experience stories from some other parts of the world, starting with India."

www.summerbridgeactivities.com  Reading Connection—Grade 6—RBP0210

## Expanding Your Reading Power

1. Check the statement that best describes the main idea of this story.

   _____ Don't let things that matter less keep you from things that matter more.

   _____ Hunger for food is the only hunger.

   _____ There is no more meaning to stories than just fun.

   _____ Milk and cookies are better than pizza and juice.

2. Check the most likely conclusion about Clio.

   _____ She is a practical joker.

   _____ She doesn't like food.

   _____ She is a student like Ben.

   _____ She is not mortal.

3. Check the phrase that best describes Clio's motivation.

   _____ She enjoys teasing people.

   _____ She wants to help people create good stories.

   _____ She wants to kidnap people to get ransom.

   _____ She is looking for a boyfriend.

## Expanding Your Word Power

Write the words from this story that have the meanings below.

1. to produce saliva _____

2. people involved in a noisy party

   _____

3. to have or become less _____

4. inspiring awe _____

5. possibilities not yet realized _____

6. successfully accomplish _____

Words that have the same sound but different spellings and meanings are called **homophones**. Write the homophones from the story for these words.

7. grate _____

8. sun _____

9. weather _____

10. seen _____

## Understanding Language

Write the words from the story that are formed by adding to these base words.

1. saliva _____

2. comfort _____

3. awe _____

4. potent _____

## Expanding Other Skills

A **thesaurus** is a reference book in which synonyms are grouped. A thesaurus can also be used to find antonyms.

1. Check the words you might look up to find synonyms for *hunger*.

   _____ desire

   _____ hunger

   _____ fasting

   _____ satisfaction

2. Check the words you might look up to find antonyms for *hunger*.

   _____ desire

   _____ hunger

   _____ fasting

   _____ satisfaction

"The five young heroes you see are brothers, descendants of King Bharata, who has died. Their cousins have stolen the kingdom from them, and they have been exiled to this wild forest for almost 12 years," Clio said.

Ben saw the brothers stalking a huge deer through the forest. Then, fatigued and extremely thirsty, they rested under a tall tree.

"Nakula, climb this tree and look for any sign of water," said Yudhistira, the eldest brother and leader of the group.

From the treetop, Nakula saw a particularly verdant area with water birds flying in and out. He told his brothers what he had seen, then headed off to find the water. He came upon the crystal-clear pond, fell to his knees, splashed water onto his face, and cupped his hands to drink.

"Stop!" a voice cried out.

Nakula glanced around, but could see no one, so he bent down to quench his overpowering thirst.

"Stop! This pond is mine, and you may not drink until you answer my questions!"

Again Nakula could see no one, so he started to drink, but as soon as the water touched his lips he fell face forward as if dead.

When Nakula did not return promptly, Yudhistira sent Sahadwa after him. Sahadwa found the sapphire blue pond without seeing the body of his brother, and he rushed down to the water's edge to drink.

"Stop!" ordered the voice. "Before you drink you must answer my questions!"

Sahadwa saw no one and bent to take a quick drink before searching for Nakula. No sooner did he bring the water to his mouth than he fell lifeless to the ground.

Arjuna was the next brother to go to the pond. He was shocked to see the bodies of Nakula and Sahadwa, and he put an arrow in his bow as he carefully crept forward. His throat and body ached for the water, so he bent for a drink.

"Stop! Do not drink of my pond until you answer my questions!"

"Here is your answer!" Arjuna shouted as he shot arrow after arrow into the surrounding forest. Finally he stopped shooting long enough to reach for some water. He, too, fell to the ground with his brothers.

Then the fourth brother, Bhima, came to the pond. His anger flared when he saw the bodies of his brothers, and he raised his mace and shouted threats to whatever evil had harmed them. There was no response until he reached into the water. Then he, too, was warned. When he ignored the warning, Bhima fell to the ground.

Yudhistira finally followed his brothers into the forest where no other men had gone before. The beauty of the enormous trees and the serene pond amazed him. But when he saw the bodies of his four brothers, his heart dropped and he was filled with anguish. He cried out, his lament echoing back from the trees, "Who has done this to my brothers? Come face me!"

## Expanding Your Reading Power

1. Number the events in the order they happened.

   _____ Yudhistira laments for his four younger brothers.

   _____ A voice warns Arjuna to answer questions before drinking.

   _____ Five brothers are exiled from their kingdom.

   _____ Nakula climbs a tree to look for water.

   _____ Bhima falls to the ground.

Circle the word that best completes this sentence.

2. Since her favorite color was blue, she chose a ring with a _____ in it.

   **emerald    ruby    sapphire    diamond**

3. Check what will most likely happen next.

   _____ Yudhistira will try to answer the questions before drinking.

   _____ Yudhistira will try to drink and fall down as if dead.

   _____ Yudhistira will fight the person who overcame his brothers.

   _____ Yudhistira will run away.

## Expanding Your Word Power

Write the words from this story that have the meanings below.

1. tracking _____

2. extremely tired _____

3. green with plants _____

4. satisfy _____

5. tranquil _____

6. expression of sorrow _____

A **metaphor** is a figurative way of saying something. For example, if you say *"She cried buckets of tears,"* you mean that someone cried lots of tears. Find the metaphor in the last paragraph. Write the metaphor and what it means.

7. _____

_____

_____

## Understanding Language

The prefix **over-** means "above" or "extremely" or "beyond." Write the meaning of each of these words.

1. overage _____

2. overcast _____

3. overcoat _____

4. overeat _____

5. overlook _____

6. overseas _____

## Expanding Other Skills

Below is a map outlining areas of south central Asia. Use an atlas, an encyclopedia, or the Internet to locate these countries and bodies of water. Write the letter of the area next to its name.

1. India _____

2. Pakistan _____

3. Afghanistan _____

4. Tibet _____

5. Arabian Sea _____

6. Nepal _____

7. Bay of Bengal _____

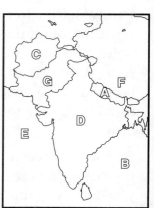

There was no answer to Yudhistira's shout. He turned to his brothers and examined the face and body of each, but found no marks of combat or discoloration, and he was mystified. He entered the pond to perform the rites for the dead, but first he bent to drink.

"Stop!" the voice called to Yudhistira. "This pond is mine! If you answer my questions, you may have water. If you can't answer them, the water is forbidden to you!"

Yudhistira's first thought was to fight, but as he thought deeper, he decided on a different course. "What god or great force are you who has vanquished my invincible brothers? I pay you homage, but I also ask humbly for an explanation for why you slew these young men when all they wanted was a drink when they were dying of thirst. Tell me, please, who you are."

The waters swirled, a mist arose, and out of the mist materialized a giant figure hovering above the pond. "I am Yaksha, the spirit who protects this part of the earth. I warned your brothers, but they ignored my warnings and tried to force their way to my water. If you would stay alive, answer my questions before you take of my water."

"Oh Yaksha, my thirst is terrible, but I will answer your questions as best as I can before I drink."

In a booming voice that filled the forest, Yaksha rapidly called out question after question, some simple, some profound. He did not give Yudhistira time to think, but Yudhistira answered just as quickly as the questions came.

"What is faster than the wind?"

"Thought."

"What sleeps with eyes open?"

"Fish."

"What remains immobile after being born?"

"Egg."

"Who is the friend of one about to die?"

"The works of charity one performed for others."

"What is one's highest duty?"

"To keep from causing injury."

As the questioning went on, Yudhistira grew weary in both body and mind, and the voice from his parched throat became hoarse and faint, until he could only whisper. Finally, Yaksha said, "Answer these last questions and I will reward you. First, how does one become agreeable?"

"By getting rid of one's pride."

"Second, how can one live without regret?"

"By getting rid of one's anger."

"Third, what is mercy?"

"Wishing happiness to all creatures."

"Which of your brothers would you choose to be revived?"

"If I have but one choice, let it be Nakula. We share the same father, but different mothers, and each mother should have one son alive."

"You please me with your humility and your thoughtful answers. You have strengthened your mind well with your learning, and I see that you are ready for the challenges ahead. Let all of your brothers rise up and join you."

With that, each of the four brothers awakened from his death trance and rejoiced with Yudhistira at their reunion.

41

## Expanding Your Reading Power

1. The story of the five Pandava brothers comes from ancient Indian writings. Check the most likely reason the original Hindu author had for telling this story.

   _____ to be funny

   _____ to teach principles of good Hindu behavior

   _____ to warn people about drinking from ponds

   _____ to tell factual history

2. Based on this story, write a **G** before statements that are Good Hindu behavior and **B** before those that are Bad Hindu behavior.

   _____ causing change through nonviolence

   _____ caring about people but not animals

   _____ helping other people

   _____ being humble

3. Check all the words that describe Yudhistira in this story.

   _____ impulsive

   _____ brave

   _____ humble

   _____ selfish

## Expanding Your Word Power

Write the words from this story that have the meanings below.

1. perplexed _____

2. religious ceremonies _____

3. defeated _____

4. honor for a person _____

5. dried _____

6. brought back to life _____

In each row, circle the two words that are related to the word in bold type.

7. **charity**
   help          love          anger

8. **duty**
   obligation    responsibility    chance

## Understanding Language

1. If the prefix **dis-** means "not," and the suffix **-tion** means "having the condition of," then what is the meaning of *discoloration*? Write a definition.

   _____

   _____

The suffix **-able** means "capable of" or "tending to." Write the **-able** words formed from these base words.

2. agree _____

3. read _____

## Expanding Other Skills

The graph shows the number of people who follow one of the world's major religions. Write the letter of the correct religion under each bar.

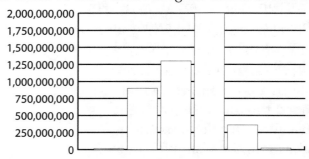

**a.** Buddhism
360,000,000

**b.** Islam
1,300,000,000

**c.** Christianity
2,000,000,000

**d.** Judaism
14,000,000

**e.** Hinduism
900,000,000

**f.** Sikhism
23,000,000

# Rabbits and Elephants

Who will win?

"I think I've got it!" Ben said, as the scene of the five happy brothers and the enchanted pond in the forest faded. "Stories give us answers. We can read stories just for fun, or we can read them for fun and for answers to things we want to understand. Sometimes those answers are simple, and sometimes they are deep."

Clio nodded. "That's good, but that's not all." She waved her hand to open up another scene. "Watch this."

A large bull elephant stood by a shrunken water hole. A bird splashed in the dregs of muddy water that remained. The elephant raised his trunk and trumpeted to gather his herd.

"The rivers are too shallow, and our ponds are dried up," the elephant said. "You must follow me to find water somewhere in the jungle closer to the mountains."

For days the elephants followed their leader through the jungle until finally they came to a beautiful pond. Excitedly they rushed into the water, not seeing the dozens of rabbit holes surrounding the large pond. After quenching their thirst, they sprayed water onto themselves and their neighbors and even rolled in the cool mud.

From behind the cover of the leaves, the rabbit king watched. As the elephants had thundered into the water, their heavy footsteps had destroyed many of the rabbit homes. If the elephants stayed, the lives of the rabbits would be ruined. Even though he was so much smaller than an elephant, he had to find a way to get the elephants to leave, so the rabbit king worked on a plan.

An elephant-sized rock stood not far from the bank, its top covered with tree branches. The rabbit king climbed to the top, hid in the leaves, and waited until the elephant king came close.

"King of the elephants, listen!" the rabbit king said in a loud voice. "Listen to the messenger of the Moon God."

The elephant king could see no one, but he asked, "What do you want?"

"The Moon God is very angry with you! He bathes in this pool every night, where the rabbits are his servants, but you elephants have scared the rabbits away!"

"We did not know," replied the elephant king. "What should we do?"

"Come back tonight, alone. When you see the Moon God shaking with anger, apologize and promise to never return to his pool!"

That night the elephant king entered the pool alone. When he looked into the water, he saw the moon reflected from the sky. His footsteps caused ripples on the surface that made the reflection of the moon shake, and he thought the Moon God was shaking with anger.

The elephant king bowed his head and apologized. "Forgive us, Moon God. We did not know this was your pool. We shall leave for another pool and never return here."

The next morning the elephants left, and the wise rabbit king and his rabbits rebuilt their homes and their lives at their pond.

www.summerbridgeactivities.com   Reading Connection—Grade 6—RBP0210

## Expanding Your Reading Power

1. Check the sentence that best states the main idea of this story.

_____ Elephants can be destructive.

_____ Sometimes mind power is more important than physical power.

_____ It's best to give in to powerful enemies.

_____ Science can explain why we see the moon in a pond.

2. Check the word that best describes this type of story.

_____ myth

_____ legend

_____ history

_____ fable

3. Write a short summary of the main action of this story.

_____

_____

_____

## Expanding Your Word Power

Write the words from this story that have the meanings below.

1. easily understood _____

2. a dangerous or difficult situation

_____

3. sediment of a liquid _____

4. gave a resounding call _____

5. small waves _____

6. mirrored image _____

Write the words from the story that are **syn-onyms** (words that have the same or similar meanings) for these words.

7. bordering _____

8. satisfying _____

## Understanding Language

Write the closed and hyphenated **compound words** formed by adding to these base words.

1. steps _____

2. sized _____

Rewrite each phrase below. Use **possessive** forms.

3. king of the rabbits _____

4. reflection of the moon _____

5. messenger of the Moon God

_____

6. lives of the rabbits _____

## Expanding Other Skills

Write the name of the best reference to use when searching for the information below.

| atlas    almanac    dictionary |
|---|
| encyclopedia    a book of fables |

1. the dates of the full moons for this year

_____

2. a map of the jungle areas of India

_____

3. stories with animals as characters

_____

4. detailed information about elephants

_____

5. the meaning of the word *enchanted*

_____

# A Weak, Skinny, Shy Boy

How did a boy become a great soul?                    The Story of Gandhi, part 1

Clio turned to Ben as the scene changed. "This is not a myth or a fable, but the story of man who actually lived. As you watch this," she said, "think about how Gandhi's life is like the story of the five brothers and the elephants and rabbits." Ben watched a man in a white shirt and tie working at an old-fashioned typewriter. The man paused from his typing to wipe either sweat or tears from his eyes. Then he pulled the paper from his typewriter. Ben read the typed paper.

## OBITUARY OF A GREAT SOUL— JANUARY 31, 1948

Yesterday a man of violence assassinated one of history's greatest symbols of peace and tolerance. Mohandas Karamchand Gandhi was about to deliver his daily prayer meeting message when he was shot. The assassin was a fellow Hindu who disagreed with Gandhi's teachings encouraging peace between Hindus and Muslims.

"The father of our nation is no more. No longer will we run to him for advice and solace," declared the Prime Minister of India in a radio address last night.

Gandhi was 78 years old, small and physically frail. He was called "Bapu" or "father" by many. More people called him "Mahatma," which means "great soul."

Gandhi was born October 2, 1869. His father was an advisor to the prince of a small state in India. Gandhi was a weak, skinny, shy boy. He was only an average student, and he often ran home after school so that the other children wouldn't tease him. As was common at the time, his family arranged a marriage for him when he was only seven. The wedding took place when he was 13.

After graduating from the University of Bombay, Gandhi studied law at University College in London, England. He returned to India in 1891 to practice law. He felt so guilty about losing his first case that he returned his client's money. He blamed his failure on his shyness before the judge.

Gandhi went to South Africa in 1893 to represent an Indian law firm. At that time, South Africa had laws restricting the rights of people based on their race. Whites had the most rights. "Coloreds," which included the large Indian population, had fewer rights. "Blacks," who were the majority population, had the fewest rights.

One of Gandhi's first experiences with racial discrimination in South Africa happened when he was riding on a train. A white passenger was upset to have a "colored" man riding in the same compartment. The conductor ordered Gandhi to third class, even though he had a first-class ticket. Gandhi refused and was thrown off the train.

Eventually, Gandhi became the first "colored" admitted to practice law before the Supreme Court of South Africa. He became wealthy from his large, successful practice. Yet Mohandas Gandhi wasn't satisfied with wealth. He started putting more and more energy into working to change South Africa's unjust laws.

His weapons in that battle were his words. Those words taught the higher principles of human rights. And nonviolence.

www.summerbridgeactivities.com

## Expanding Your Reading Power

1. Check the words that describe Gandhi.

   _____ determined

   _____ boastful

   _____ well-educated

   _____ greedy

2. Write **F** for each statement of fact. Write **O** for each statement of opinion.

   _____ Gandhi was the greatest man in India.

   _____ Gandhi became a wealthy lawyer.

   _____ Gandhi influenced millions.

   _____ Gandhi was too young when he got married.

3. What do you think the phrase "the father of our nation" might mean?

   _____

   _____

## Expanding Your Word Power

Write the words from this story that have the meanings below.

1. respect for others _____

2. comfort in distress _____

3. slight, weak _____

4. customer _____

5. keeping within limits _____

6. rules of behavior _____

Write the words or phrases from the story that could be represented by these abbreviations.

7. PM_____

8. U of B_____

9. UCL _____

10. SCSA _____

## Understanding Language

The suffix **-tion** means "have the condition of, or being in the state of." Write the words from the story that have the suffix **-tion** and are formed from these base words.

1. connect _____

2. populate _____

3. discriminate _____

The word root **-graph-** means "write, or writing." Write the meanings of these words.

4. biography (*bio* means "life")

   _____

5. autograph (*auto* means "self")

   _____

6. photograph (*photo* means "light")

   _____

7. geography (*geo* means "earth")

   _____

## Expanding Other Skills

Read this train ticket and answer the questions.

| Passenger Name | | | | Date of Issue |
|---|---|---|---|---|
| Gandhi, M.K. | | | | 12 Oct. 1893 |
| | Train No. | Class | Date | Time |
| From: Durban | 8205 | First Class | 13 Oct. 1893 | Dep. 8:10 A.M. |
| To: Johannesburg | 8205 | First Class | 14 Oct. 1893 | Arv. 4:22 P.M. |

1. When was the ticket issued?

   _____

2. Who is the passenger?

   _____

3. Where is the passenger going?

   _____

4. What class did the passenger buy?

   _____

5. How long will the trip take?

   _____

Gandhi visited India in 1896 and wrote a pamphlet about discrimination in South Africa. His pamphlet angered many whites in South Africa. When he returned to South Africa an angry mob beat him.

That was a turning point for Gandhi. After that beating, Gandhi started a movement to fight for human rights. He believed no one should injure anyone else.

Gandhi and his followers refused to obey unjust laws. He was jailed many times because of that. In jail, he studied the teachings of Jesus, Thoreau, and Tolstoy. He also wrote and prayed.

After a few years, some of the laws were changed. Gandhi was a hero to the Indians in South Africa.

After 20 years in South Africa, Gandhi returned to India. He wanted freedom for his homeland, India, which had been part of the British Empire since 1757.

Gandhi helped the freedom movement grow. Four years after Gandhi returned, the government passed a law to prohibit organizing against the government. Thousands of Indians gathered in a peaceful protest against that law. British soldiers opened fire on the crowd. They killed 379 people and wounded more than 1,200 others.

Gandhi responded to that tragic confrontation by organizing a boycott of the government and foreign goods. Thousands of Indians quit their government jobs. They took their children out of government schools. Gandhi wanted his people to work in home industries instead of working for foreign companies. He wanted his people to weave their own cloth instead of buying cloth from England. He used a spinning wheel and loom to make cloth for his own clothes. From then on, he wore only a loincloth and shawl he had made.

Salt was important in the Indian diet. The British government controlled the salt trade and taxed its sale. In 1930, 60-year-old Gandhi walked 241 miles to the Arabian Sea. It took 24 days. He started his march with 78 followers, but ended it with thousands. They gathered seawater in clay pots and then put the pots in the sun. When the water evaporated, they had salt.

Gandhi was arrested because he made his own salt. His people followed his example. Eventually 60,000 of his followers were also arrested. The British could not keep jailing so many people, so they made some changes to the laws.

Meanwhile, Gandhi's fame grew throughout the world. In 1930, *Time* magazine named Gandhi "Man of the Year."

Gandhi also worked to end the injustices of India's "caste" system. This system divided people into classes and gave more privileges to Indians born in upper-caste families.

Some Indians resented Gandhi for his work against the caste system. Others resented him for his work to end hostilities between Hindus and Muslims. But the vast majority of Indians revered Gandhi as a great soul.

When Gandhi fasted to protest injustices, millions grew concerned for his life. Change often resulted.

The greatest change took place when Britain granted independence to India in 1947. India won that freedom by a revolution of nonviolence led by a frail little man named Gandhi.

## Expanding Your Reading Power

1. Number the events in the order they happened.

   _____ Millions of Indians follow Gandhi's nonviolent revolution.

   _____ India becomes part of the British Empire.

   _____ India becomes a free country.

   _____ Gandhi is assassinated.

2. Check the likely conclusions about Gandhi.

   _____ Gandhi lived Hindu and other principles of nonviolence.

   _____ Gandhi probably studied the stories of the Pandava brothers.

   _____ Gandhi was not intimidated by the power of the British Empire.

   _____ Gandhi led by example.

3. Why did the Indians, and others in the world, have so much respect for Gandhi?

   _____

   _____

4. List three nonviolent ways Gandhi and his followers protested.

   a. _____

   b. _____

   c. _____

## Expanding Your Word Power

Write the words from this story that have the meanings below.

1. a short book _____

2. unfair treatment _____

3. a machine for weaving _____

4. an exclusive social class _____

5. actions against an enemy

   _____

Write the **antonyms** from the story for these words.

6. allow _____

7. support _____

## Understanding Language

Write the words from the story that are formed from these base words.

1. just _____

2. vapor _____

3. depend _____

Write the compound words from the story that answer these clues.

4. place of a person's birth _____

5. a simple garment _____

6. what oceans are made of _____

The word root **-liber-** means "free." Write the meanings of these words.

7. liberty _____

8. liberate _____

## Expanding Other Skills

English has adopted words from many languages. Using a dictionary, write a definition for each of these words adopted from India.

1. bungalow _____

2. cot _____

3. guru _____

4. karma _____

5. shampoo _____

# Talking Chiefs and Griots

Why are these storytellers so important?

As Ben finished reading Gandhi's obituary, the scene faded away. He sat thinking for a minute; then he turned to Clio.

"Gandhi got his ideas from reading the stories and ideas other people had written," he said. "The answers that the oldest brother gave to the spirit of the pond were the Hindu ideas that Gandhi used. And Gandhi was small and weak, like a rabbit, and the British had armies like big, strong elephants, but Gandhi got them to leave the pond of his people."

"Very good," said Clio.

"So, when the great ideas in stories are written down, they can be passed on over hundreds or even thousands of years."

"That's true, but not all people had written language."

Clio opened up a new scene. An elderly, brown-skinned man stood under a coconut tree speaking to a circle of people sitting cross-legged on woven mats. He had a bare chest and bare feet and wore a skirt-like lavalava made of finely woven pandanus strips. A braided flywhisk was draped across his shoulder, and he held a tall staff.

Ben listened as the man spoke to the people.

"Stones decay, but words last," he said.

"Welcome to Samoa," Clio said. "This is the talking chief, Leausa. For hundreds of years, Samoans had no written language. The talking chiefs memorized the stories, histories, proverbs, and genealogies of the people. Samoa wasn't the only place where this happened, either."

Quickly the scene faded to West Africa, where Ben saw men speaking in front of gatherings of people. Some of them accompanied themselves with stringed instruments or drums. A few of them talked directly to Ben.

"We are griots," one man said. "We are the memory of our people; by the spoken word we bring to life the deeds and exploits of kings for younger generations."

Another griot spoke. "The singing that comes from the heart will echo in the ear of your children and live on in your people."

A third griot approached Ben. "What kind of people we become depends on the stories on which we are nurtured."

This griot sat next to Ben. "Griots are born to the griot caste, but only children who show talent are trained. As apprentices, they make and repair the musical instruments and they memorize, memorize, memorize. A griot is like a living library of history, traditions, songs, and stories. It can take 50 years to know enough to be a master.

"Each griot's performance is different because the griot has the people in the audience get involved. They all become part of telling a story."

He pointed to a brightly dressed woman standing in front of a group of children and their families. "That is my wife, Fatou, who is a griotte. We have been in charge of the entertainment for a wedding. Listen as she tells two stories about Anansi, the spiderman."

www.summerbridgeactivities.com **Reading Connection—Grade 6—RBP0210**

## Expanding Your Reading Power

1. Check the statement that best expresses the main idea of this story.

    _____ Gandhi learned important lessons from stories.

    _____ Samoa has different kinds of chiefs.

    _____ Much of Africa did not have a written language.

    _____ Preserving stories was important even when there was no written language.

2. Write **W** before the statements that describe only written stories. Write **O** before the statements that describe only oral stories. Write **WO** before statements that describe both.

    _____ Stories can teach important lessons.

    _____ Stories keep the exact same words.

    _____ An audience can change a story.

    _____ Music is often involved.

3. Write your own explanation for this quote: "Stones decay, but words last."

    _____

    _____

    _____

## Expanding Your Word Power

Write the words from this story that have the meanings below.

1. notice of death _____

2. noteworthy deeds _____

3. very importantly _____

4. developed, nourished _____

5. those learning a trade or profession

Write the words from the story that are **homophones** (words with the same sound but different spellings and meanings) for these words.

6. week _____

7. past _____

8. bear _____

## Understanding Language

Rewrite each of the three hyphenated **compound words** from this story as a phrase.

1. _____

2. _____

3. _____

The word root **-gen-** means "birth, kind, origin." Use a dictionary to define these words.

4. genealogy _____

5. genetic _____

6. genuine _____

## Expanding Other Skills

Use the map of Africa to answer the questions.

1. Griots were found among the Mandingo, Ashanti, Fulani, Hausa, and Yoruba people. Where in Africa did they live?

    _____

    _____

2. Would west Africa, south Africa, or east Africa have been closest for slave traders going to the Americas?

    _____

# Anansi and the Pot of Wisdom

Where does wisdom come from?

A long, long time ago, at the beginning of the world, people could not solve their problems. Nyame, the sky god, looked down and felt sorry for them. So he said, "I will send down wisdom to the people, and then they can solve their problems."

Now it just so happened that Anansi, the spiderman, was visiting Nyame that day, and he heard what Nyame planned to do.

"That is a splendid idea!" said Anansi. "Give the wisdom to me, and I will take it down to the people."

Now, do you think Nyame should trust that selfish trickster with his wisdom? Nevertheless, Nyame put his wisdom in a big clay pot and gave it to Anansi. "This wisdom is more valuable than gold or silver or any other thing," said Nyame. "Take this to the people so they can solve their problems."

Anansi took the pot down to the earth and looked inside. It was full of wonderful ideas and skills. "I will use this wisdom first," he said to himself, "before I give it to the people."

Each day Anansi opened the pot and learned new things. "There is so much wisdom in here," he said. "I must keep it a long time before I give it to the people."

After many days, Anansi said, "This wisdom is too valuable to share with people. I must keep it for myself." So he decided to hide it in the top of a high tree where a spiderman could climb but no person could go. But how could he carry such a heavy pot up the tree?

Anansi had an idea. He gathered some strong vines, tied them around the pot, then tied the other end around his waist and started to climb. But the dangling pot kept getting in his way and catching in the branches.

Anansi's son came by and saw his father's struggles and frustration. "Father," the young boy said, "if you tie the pot to your back it will be much easier for you to hold onto the tree and climb."

Anansi followed his son's advice and switched the pot to his back. The rest of the climb was much easier, but when he got to the top and looked back down at his little son, he thought, "What a fool I am! I have the pot of wisdom, and yet a little boy had more common sense than I did! What use is all this wisdom to me?"

In a fit of anger, Anansi threw the pot down to the ground where it smashed into millions of pieces, and the wisdom scattered all over the world. People found the bits of wisdom and took them home to their families. And that is why to this day no one person has all of the wisdom, and that is why we each share a piece of our wisdom with each other when we exchange ideas.

© RBP Books    www.summerbridgeactivities.com    Reading Connection—Grade 6—RBP0210

## Expanding Your Reading Power

1. Check the most likely reason a griot would have for telling this story.

   _____ to entertain

   _____ to persuade

   _____ to give factual information

2. Check all the words that describe Anansi in this story.

   _____ selfish

   _____ trustworthy

   _____ sneaky

   _____ humble

3. Check the word that best describes the mood of this story.

   _____ tense

   _____ humorous

   _____ scary

4. Check the word that best describes this type of story.

   _____ myth

   _____ novel

   _____ history

   _____ epic

## Expanding Your Word Power

Write the words from this story that have the meanings below.

1. magnificent _____

2. deceiver _____

3. hanging loosely _____

4. discouraged feelings _____

5. dispersed _____

6. give and receive _____

7. Check the sentence in which *rest* has the same meaning as in paragraph 10.

   _____ She wanted to hear the rest of the story.

   _____ He decided to lie down for a rest.

   _____ Rest the ladder against the wall.

8. Check the sentence in which *fit* has the same meaning as in paragraph 11.

   _____ The dress was a perfect fit.

   _____ Can you fit me into your schedule?

   _____ She expected him to have a fit when she said, "No."

## Understanding Language

The prefix **inter-** means "between" or "among." Match the words that have the prefix **inter-** with the meanings below.

| a. interfere | b. international | c. intersection |
|---|---|---|
| d. interview | e. interrupt | f. interact |

1. _____ a face-to-face meeting

2. _____ meddle

3. _____ to act on each other

4. _____ place where two things cross

5. _____ break into an activity

6. _____ among many nations

## Expanding Other Skills

**Entry words** of different kinds can be found in dictionaries. Match the entry type with the correct example.

1. _____ abbreviation

2. _____ idiom

3. _____ prefix

4. _____ proper noun

5. _____ suffix

| a. Africa |
| b. in- |
| c. a.m. |
| d. -ward |
| e. far-fetched |

# Anansi and All the Stories (part 1)

How would you capture hornets, a snake, and a leopard?

When Anansi, the spiderman, had the pot of all wisdom, he learned some things, but he didn't learn all things. Mostly he wanted to learn to be clever, and cleverness he did learn. Another thing he learned was that Nyame, the sky god, had another great treasure—stories. The stories taught other things, like the beginnings and endings of everything. Nyame kept all the stories hidden away in a big wooden box.

Anansi climbed up through the clouds to Nyame and asked him for his stories. Nyame laughed and said, "Anansi, my stories are very valuable and many creatures more wealthy and powerful than you have sought to have them, but no creature has been able to give me what I ask in return for them. What makes you think you can earn my stories?"

"Sometimes it is better to be clever than to be rich or powerful. Tell me your price for your stories, and I will get it for you."

"Very well, then. My price is that you bring me three fearsome creatures. First, Mmoboro, the hornets with the terrible sting. Second, Onini, the python that swallows men whole. Third, Osebo, the leopard with knives for claws and spear points for teeth."

Anansi bowed to Nyame and said, "I shall return with your fearsome creatures." Then he climbed back down through the clouds.

Anansi thought and thought as he devised his plans. Then, when he was ready, he went into action. First, he went to his garden to cut two old, dry gourds and a large banana leaf. He cut holes in the ends of the gourds and filled one of them with water from the river, where he also drenched himself. Soaking wet, he went to the tree where Mmoboro, the hornets lived, and poured the water from the gourd onto the hornets in their home so they could barely fly.

"Mmoboro," he called, as he held the banana leaf over his head, as if protecting himself from rain. "Do not be foolish. Get out of this rain!"

"But where can we go?" buzzed the hornets.

"Fly into this dry gourd."

When the hornets had flown into the gourd, Anansi plugged up the hole with a wad of grass.

"Foolish, indeed," he murmured, as he climbed up through the clouds to Nyame.

"Nicely done," said Nyame, "but the reward is not paid until the task is completed."

Anansi went back down through the clouds to work on his second plan. This time he must capture Onini, the python who swallows men whole. But how?

www.summerbridgeactivities.com    **Reading Connection—Grade 6—RBP0210**

## Expanding Your Reading Power

1. Check the reasons Anansi was able to capture Mmoboro.

   _____ Mmoboro trusted Anansi.

   _____ Anansi was stronger than Mmoboro.

   _____ Mmoboro do not want to be wet.

   _____ Anansi had devised a good plan.

2. Write **T** before statements that are true. Write **F** before statements that are false.

   _____ Only Nyame and Anansi knew about the stories.

   _____ Nyame lived in the sky.

   _____ Little creatures, like hornets, cannot hurt people.

   _____ Anansi had confidence.

3. Check what will most likely happen next in this story.

   _____ Anansi will beat Onini with a bamboo pole.

   _____ Anansi will capture Onini and take him to Nyame.

   _____ Onini will defeat Anansi.

   _____ Anansi's wife will capture Onini.

## Expanding Your Word Power

Write the words from this story that have the meanings below.

1. frightening _____

2. invent _____

3. fruits related to pumpkins and squashes

   _____

4. soaked _____

5. saturated _____

6. small mass of soft material

   _____

Write two **metaphors** from paragraph 4.

7. _____

8. _____

## Understanding Language

1. The suffix **-ish** means "having the qualities of," "tending to," or "somewhat." Write the word from the story with the suffix **–ish**. Write a definition of the word.

   _____

   _____

Write definitions for these words.

2. greenish_____

3. selfish_____

4. sheepish_____

5. devilish _____

## Expanding Other Skills

Complete this outline for paragraph 4.

   I. Three fearsome creatures

     A. Mmoboro

       1. hornets _____

       2. terrible sting _____

     B. Onini

       1. _____

       2. _____

     C. Osebo

       1. _____

       2. _____

       3. _____

Have you ever played a clever trick?

To pay the sky god's price for all the world's stories, Anansi next had to capture Onini, the python who swallows men whole. So Anansi cut a long, thick bamboo pole and walked into the swampy area where Onini lived. As he walked, he argued with himself, saying, "No, I am sure I am right. He is longer than this branch. But she says shorter. No, definitely longer."

Onini came up to Anansi and said, "Why are you talking like this to yourself?"

"I had an argument with my wife about you," Anansi said. "My wife says you are shorter than this bamboo pole, and I say a powerful snake like you must be much longer. It has been a terrible argument, and we can't solve it."

"That's easy," said Onini. "Put down the pole, and I will lie next to it. Then you can see that I am longer."

Anansi put the pole on the ground and Onini slithered next to it, but try as he might, he could not stretch longer than the branch.

"You are too slippery to straighten out to your great, full length," said Anansi. "Let me tie your head to one end of the pole, and then you can stretch out your tail past the other end."

Onini agreed, so Anansi used a strong vine to tie Onini's head to one end of the bamboo pole. The python stretched out his tail, which Anansi tied to the other end. Then he fastened Onini's body to the branch and carried him up through the clouds, murmuring, "Foolish, indeed."

"Nicely done," said Nyame, "but the reward is not paid until the task is completed."

Anansi went back down through the clouds to work on his third plan. He went to the forest where Osebo, the leopard with claws like knives and teeth like spear points, lived. He found Osebo's path, and while the leopard was asleep, he dug a deep pit and covered the opening with a thin layer of sticks and leaves. When Osebo prowled the forest path that night, he fell in and, try as he might, he could not jump or climb out.

"What are you doing in that hole, Osebo?" Anansi asked the next morning.

"I've fallen in this trap, Anansi. Help me to get out."

Anansi bent a strong, green sapling over the hole and tied it to a sturdy tree trunk. Then he tied another vine to the sapling and lowered the end down to Osebo. "Tie that vine to your tail," Anansi said, "and make sure it is tight."

When Anansi could see that Osebo had tied the vine to his tail, he cut the vine holding the sapling to the tree trunk. The sapling sprung up, yanking Osebo out of the hole and spinning the leopard around and around until he was so dizzy that Anansi could bind up his feet and mouth with yet another vine.

"Foolish, indeed," Anansi murmured as he took Osebo through the clouds to Nyame.

"Nicely done," said Nyame. "Now the task is completed, and your reward shall be paid."

Nyame called together his nobles and had his wooden box of stories brought forth. "With his cleverness, Anansi has done what others could not do with riches and power. Forever more, all the sky god's stories belong to Anansi, and anyone who spins a good story owes a reward to the spiderman."

## Expanding Your Reading Power

1. Write **M** before statements that describe Mmoboro. Write **ON** before statements that describe Onini. Write **OS** before statements that describe Osebo.

    _____ has powerful legs

    _____ work together in a colony

    _____ swallows animals whole

    _____ disabled by rain

2. Check the statements that best explain why Anansi stories were so popular.

    _____ Clever solutions to problems can be entertaining.

    _____ They were the only stories the people had.

    _____ Anansi was a real person.

    _____ The stories are fun ways to teach morals.

3. Write a short summary of the main action in the two parts of this story.

    _____

    _____

    _____

## Expanding Your Word Power

Write the words from this story that have the meanings below.

1. moved by slipping and sliding

    _____

2. roamed while searching for prey

    _____

3. young tree _____

4. pulling suddenly _____

5. having a whirling sensation; unbalanced

    _____

6. tie or restrain _____

In each row below, circle the two words that are related.

7. sturdy          flimsy          solid

8. cricket          python          reptile

## Understanding Language

The prefix **a-** means "without or opposite," "on or in," "up, out, or away," or "of or from." Write words with the prefix *a-* that have these meanings:

1. sleeping _____

2. on board _____

3. going by foot _____

4. round about _____

## Expanding Other Skills

Check the words you might look up in a thesaurus to find synonyms for these words.

1. *leopard*

    _____ animal

    _____ fish

    _____ insect

    _____ horse

2. *sapling*

    _____ plant

    _____ spring

    _____ vitamin

    _____ tree

3. *story*

    _____ complaint

    _____ length

    _____ place

    _____ drama

# Lil' Dotta and Brer Rabby

Do you know any Brer Rabby stories?

"When African stories came to the United States, sometimes the trickster changed from a spider to a rabbit," said Clio.

Brer Rabby was the slyest animal in the woods. Every day he watched Daddy go off to work and Mama take a big basket of vegetables to sell at the market. But Lil' Dotta stayed home to watch the house and tend the garden. And what a garden it was—tomatoes, greens, cucumbers, okra, beans, and, best of all, long rows of the sweetest green peas ever. Brer Rabby especially had a taste for those sweet green peas, but there was no hole in the fence that even a rabbit could squeeze through.

One morning after Daddy and Mama left, Brer Rabby hopped up to the fence. "Good morning, Lil' Dotta!" he said, all cheerful. "Your Mama just said to me, 'Tell Lil' Dotta to let you in for some of those fine peas.'"

So Lil' Dotta opened the gate, and in no time that long-eared, big-footed rabbit ate up a whole row of those tender, young peas and then left.

Mama got home, and was she ever surprised at that sneaky rabbit tricking Lil' Dotta. "Tomorrow, if Brer Rabby comes back, you let him in, but don't let him back out. When your Daddy gets home, he'll take care of that pesky animal."

The next day, Daddy and Mama left, and sure enough, Brer Rabby hopped up to the gate and told Lil' Dotta that Mama had said to let him in. Lil' Dotta did just that, only this time she locked the gate behind him. When Brer Rabby's round belly was so full it was almost dragging on the ground, he asked Lil' Dotta to let him out.

"I'm busy right now, Brer Rabby," she said. The whole day long, Lil' Dotta was busy, and no matter how much Brer Rabby begged and pleaded, she told him he would have to wait.

When Daddy got home, he caught Brer Rabby by the ears, stuffed him in a gunnysack, and hung that gunnysack on a tree. Then Daddy and Lil' Dotta went to the woods to cut a switch.

While they were gone, Brer Fox happened by the wiggling bag. "Who's in that sack and how come?" he asked.

Brer Rabby was thinking fast. "It's me, Brer Rabby, and I'm going to heaven for Lil' Dotta. You want to come along?"

"Why sure!" Brer Fox answered. But when he untied the gunnysack to climb in, Brer Rabby jumped out and tied old Brer Fox inside.

Daddy brought back the switch to whoop Brer Rabby and teach him a lesson. He opened the gunnysack, and what a surprise to find Brer Fox! Brer Fox was all mad and flustered when he explained what happened.

"That sneaky rabbit sure is a sly one!" Daddy said to Lil' Dotta, and they laughed and laughed.

© RBP Books    www.summerbridgeactivities.com    Reading Connection—Grade 6—RBP0210

## Expanding Your Reading Power

1. Check the words that best describe Brer Rabby.
   _____ trustworthy
   _____ sneaky
   _____ truthful
   _____ clever

2. Write **F** before each statement of fact. Write **O** before each statement of opinion.
   _____ Okra is the best vegetable.
   _____ Rabbits can talk only in stories.
   _____ Brer Rabby was smarter than Lil' Dotta.
   _____ Using a switch is good discipline.

3. Number the events in the order they happened.
   _____ Brer Rabby lied to Lil' Dotta to get to the peas.
   _____ Daddy and Lil' Dotta were surprised to find Brer Fox in the gunnysack.
   _____ Daddy caught Brer Rabby and put him in a gunnysack.
   _____ Brer Rabby lied to Brer Fox.

## Expanding Your Word Power

Write the words from this story that have the meanings below.

1. cunning _____

2. tall plant with sticky, edible pods
   _____

3. implored _____

4. sack made of burlap _____

5. confused _____

6. Check the sentence in which *switch* has the same meaning as in paragraph 12.
   _____ He cut a long, thin willow switch.
   _____ She wants to switch the subject.
   _____ Switch off the television.

## Understanding Language

Rewrite each phrase below with possessives.

1. story of the grandmother
   _____

2. gate of the fence
   _____

The suffix **-ster** means "a person who is, does, or creates." Write definitions for these words:

3. trickster _____

4. oldster _____

5. youngster _____

## Expanding Other Skills

Here is a recipe for pizza with a southern flavor.

| Recipe for Shrimp and Okra Pizza | |
|---|---|
| 1 pre-baked pizza crust | ⅓ c green pepper, sliced |
| 1 jar pizza sauce | 1 c okra, sliced |
| 3-6 drops hot sauce | 1 c cooked shrimp |
| 1 c cheddar cheese | 1 tomato, chopped |
| ⅓ c onion, chopped | 1 c mozzarella cheese |

1. Is this more likely a recipe from modern times or from before the Civil War? Why?
   _____
   _____

2. Which ingredients are not typical of pizza?
   _____
   _____

# Hidden Meanings
Did you know songs helped slaves escape to the North?

Brer Rabby hopped up to Ben and stood on his hind legs. Then suddenly he started growing taller and changing, and within a few seconds, he had morphed into a tall, broad-shouldered man who was grinning down at Ben.

"My name's James," he said in a deep, resonant voice. "I was a slave before the Civil War, before I escaped to the North. Stories helped me get my freedom. There were the stories of clever people who could get the best of people with more power and the stories of slaves who had gone on the Underground Railroad and made it to freedom. Those stories made me feel I could do it, too. Some of those stories were in songs. Did you ever think of songs as stories?"

"No, not really," said Ben.

"Well, most of them are, and some of them are stories that say one thing but mean something else at the same time. We had a lot of songs like that, and the masters didn't know we were learning two things in one song.

"A carpenter named Peg Leg Joe traveled through Alabama and Mississippi, working on plantations and teaching slaves a song called 'Follow the Drinking Gourd.' The drinking gourd was really the Big Dipper in the night sky, and the song had a secret code giving directions to the North.

"Only a few slaves could read or write, but it was easy to memorize songs, and we knew that getting to the Promised Land, or heaven, could also mean getting to the North. 'Wade through the Water' was about baptism when you looked at it one way, or troubles in life if you looked at it another way. But it also taught us to go a long ways in the streams and rivers so the bloodhounds would lose our scent.

"Ben, you listen to this song with your ears and your heart and see if you can uncover the secret code."

James sang softly in a voice full of passion:

*Swing low, sweet chariot,*
*Coming for to carry me home,*
*Swing low, sweet chariot,*
*Coming for to carry me home.*

*I looked over Jordan and what did I see,*
*Coming for to carry me home,*
*A band of angels coming after me,*
*Coming for to carry me home.*

*If you get there before I do,*
*Coming for to carry me home,*
*Tell all my friends I'm coming, too,*
*Coming for to carry me home.*

*The brightest day that ever I saw,*
*Coming for to carry me home,*
*When Jesus washed my sins away,*
*Coming for to carry me home.*

*I'm sometimes up and sometimes down,*
*Coming for to carry me home,*
*But still, my soul feels heavenly bound,*
*Coming for to carry me home.*

*Swing low, sweet chariot,*
*Coming for to carry me home,*
*Swing low, sweet chariot,*
*Coming for to carry me home.*

© RBP Books        www.summerbridgeactivities.com        Reading Connection—Grade 6—RBP0210

## Expanding Your Reading Power

1. Check the statement that best expresses the main idea of this story.

   _____ Some people treated slaves well.

   _____ Bloodhounds tracked runaways.

   _____ Stars are good for finding directions at night.

   _____ Some slave songs had hidden meanings.

A **symbol** is an object that represents something else. Check the closest meaning for these symbols from the song.

2. *chariot*

   _____ the underground railroad

   _____ a horse and buggy

   _____ a funeral wagon

3. *Jordan*

   _____ clouds

   _____ the dividing line, especially rivers, between the North and the South

   _____ a country in the Middle East

4. *angels*

   _____ children

   _____ slave trackers

   _____ people who helped slaves escape

5. *home*

   _____ the free states

   _____ death

   _____ the original slave owner's place

## Expanding Your Word Power

Write the words from this story that have the meanings below.

1. changed from one form to another

   _____

2. full and resounding _____

3. secret organization _____

4. a farm with workers living on it

   _____

5. large dogs that track by scent

   _____

6. wheeled cart drawn by horses

   _____

Write the words from the story that are **antonyms** (words that have the opposite meaning) for these words.

7. emotionless _____

8. forget _____

## Understanding Language

Write the **compound words** from the story that are made by adding to these base words.

1. ground _____

2. road _____

3. hound _____

## Expanding Other Skills

Below is a map showing some of the free states and slave states before the Civil War.

1. Use an atlas. Which rivers formed part of this boundary?

   _____

   _____

2. Approximately how far would a person have to travel to go from the northern border of North Carolina to get to a free state?

   _____

## What do you know about Martin Luther King Jr.?

James had a faraway look in his eyes when he finished singing "Swing Low, Sweet Chariot." "It wasn't easy, getting up to the North," he said, "getting past the bloodhounds and the slave hunters. But I got there, and freedom was so sweet. And then I was wondering about my family and my friends, and I knew I had to try to help anyone else escaping to the North. So I went back into the South. I made a few trips before I was caught. I never got away again."

"That's like my people. President Lincoln gave us our freedom, but then others found ways to take some of that freedom away with new laws and in other ways. Can we show Ben what I mean?"

Clio opened up a new scene. Ben saw a young boy and his mother standing in front of a drinking fountain. A sign above the foundtain read "Whites Only."

"That young man was born in 1929, more than 65 years after Lincoln's Emancipation Proclamation ended slavery. His name was Martin Luther King, Jr."

The "Whites Only" signs bothered Martin. His mother told him the signs came from unjust laws that needed to be changed because the color of a person's skin had nothing to do with how good or bad the person might be.

Ben saw Martin in church listening to his father preach. Martin wanted to become a preacher like his father, to use big words to help change the unjust laws. So Martin applied himself to his schooling, learning big ideas to go with the big words. He discovered the writings of Mahatma Gandhi and was impressed that Gandhi used nonviolence to help gain freedom for millions of people in India.

Martin received a doctoral degree in 1955 when he was 26 years old. That same year, an African American woman named Rosa Parks sat down in the "Whites Only" area of a public bus in Montgomery, Alabama. When she refused to give up her seat, she was arrested. Martin helped the African American people of Montgomery organize a boycott of the buses. For more than a year, people walked or set up car pools for rides, until finally change began to come.

Dr. King continued his fight to make laws just for all people regardless of race. Like Gandhi, he went to jail rather than obey unjust laws. He led by example, and he motivated people through his speeches and his writings. Then Ben saw Dr. King standing on the steps of the Lincoln Memorial in Washington, D.C., in front of thousands of people. Dr. King spoke into the microphone, delivering one of his most famous speeches, "I Have a Dream."

## Expanding Your Reading Power

1. Check the words that describe Dr. Martin Luther King Jr.

   _____ brave

   _____ violent

   _____ educated

   _____ determined

2. List three things that influenced Dr. King to work nonviolently to change unjust laws.

   a. _____

   b. _____

   c. _____

3. Write **T** before statements that are true. Write **F** before statements that are false.

   _____ Martin Luther King Sr. was a preacher.

   _____ Martin Luther King Jr. studied the life and writings of Gandhi.

   _____ The bus boycott in Alabama lasted only one month.

   _____ Martin Luther King Jr. and Gandhi never went to jail.

## Expanding Your Word Power

Write the words from this story that have the meanings below.

1. freedom from bondage _____

2. public announcement _____

3. a high degree from a university

   _____

4. not using or buying as a protest

   _____

5. a shady public walk _____

Write the words from the story that are **synonyms** (words that have the same or similar meanings) for these words.

6. prison_____

7. journeys_____

## Understanding Language

Write the **compound word** from the story that is formed by adding to this base word.

1. away _____

The prefix **non-** means "not." Write the meaning of each of these words.

2. nonviolent _____

3. nonprofit_____

4. nonsense _____

5. nonfiction_____

6. nonstop_____

## Expanding Other Skills

Many words have multiple meanings. Dictionaries number the definitions for each entry. With the help of a dictionary, write two meanings for each word below.

1. degree

   a. _____

      _____

   b. _____

      _____

2. back

   a. _____

      _____

   b. _____

      _____

# "I Have a Dream"

What makes a speech effective?

A man standing next to Ben had a tear in his eye. When Dr. Martin Luther King Jr. paused in his speech, the man called out, "Right on!"

Dr. King continued, "I say to you today, my friends, that in spite of the difficulties and frustrations of the moment, I still have a dream. It is a dream deeply rooted in the American Dream. I have a dream that one day this nation will rise up and live out the true meaning of its creed: 'We hold these truths to be self-evident: that all men are created equal.'"

As Dr. King spoke of the sons of former slaves and former slaveowners joining in brotherhood, Ben glanced around the crowd. African Americans and whites stood next to each other. Some even held hands. More than 250,000 people were packed together, excited and eager to listen. Ben had learned about this speech in history, and he could hardly believe he was here. It was August 28, 1963.

Dr. King's voice boomed through the sound system as he spoke of a place "sweltering with the heat of injustice and oppression" that would be "transformed into an oasis of freedom and justice." Next to Ben stood a family whose young daughter was listening to the speech while sitting on her daddy's shoulders. On the steps of the Lincoln Memorial, Dr. King was talking about his own children.

"I have a dream that my four little children will one day live in a nation where they will not be judged by the color of their skin but by the content of their character," Dr.

King said. The little girl's father nodded and clapped his hands.

Then Ben recognized the words to "America the Beautiful" that he had learned in school: "My country 'tis of thee, sweet land of liberty, of thee I sing. Land where my fathers died, land of the Pilgrims' pride, from every mountainside, let freedom ring!'" He hadn't thought about what the words of the song had meant before, but they seemed important now. Ben felt his emotions rising with the people in the crowd as men and women shouted in agreement.

"Let freedom ring," Dr. King proclaimed, "from the prodigious hilltops of New Hampshire" and the "Alleghenies of Pennsylvania" to the "snow-capped Rockies of Colorado" and the "peaks of California."

The father next to Ben seemed to be leaning forward, while his little girl gripped his shirt. Ben felt his body tingle as Dr. King finished.

"When we let freedom ring, when we let it ring from every village and every hamlet, from every state and every city, we will be able to speed up that day when all of God's children, black men and white men, Jews and Gentiles, Protestants and Catholics, will be able to join hands and sing in the words of the old Negro spiritual, 'Free at last! Free at last! Thank God Almighty, we are free at last.'"

"Free at last!
Free at last!

## Expanding Your Reading Power

1. Check the likely reasons Dr. King had for writing and delivering this speech.

    _____ to entertain

    _____ to help people understand changes that needed to be made

    _____ to divide the people of America

    _____ to encourage people who were working for civil rights

Write the words that best complete each sentence.

2. The Lincoln Memorial was _____ into a stage.

    creed          packed          transformed

3. All the citizens resented the _____ of the dictator.

    kindness      oppression      wardrobe

4. Check the words that best describe the mood of this speech.

    _____ passionate

    _____ humorous

    _____ boring

    _____ motivational

## Expanding Your Word Power

Write the words from this story that have the meanings below.

1. affected by high heat _____

2. a fertile green spot in a desert _____

3. a buzzing, ticklish feeling _____

4. amazing; a large amount _____

5. a set of beliefs _____

6. small village _____

Write the full names of the states mentioned in the story that have these abbreviations.

7. CA _____

8. PA _____

## Understanding Language

Write the closed and hyphenated compound words from the story that have these meanings.

1. obvious by itself _____

2. owners of slaves _____

3. the side of a mountain _____

4. the tops of hills _____

5. with snow on top _____

## Expanding Other Skills

A card catalog in a library and search engines on a computer give you different ways of searching for information, such as by author, title, or subject. Read this card catalog reference and answer the questions below.

> **I Have a Dream: The Life and Words of Martin Luther King, Jr.**
>
> by Haskins, James, 1941–
> Millbrook Press, © 1992.
> Call #: 92 K53h

1. What is the title of the book?

    _____

2. What is the subject?

    _____

3. What year was the book copyrighted and published? _____

4. How would you find the book on the shelf? _____

# Would You Like to Tell Stories?

What opportunities could you find to tell stories?

The scene with Dr. King faded, and Ben saw Clio standing next to James.

"James had a great-granddaughter you are going to meet now," Clio said. "Her name is Dorothy. She used to be a librarian, but now she is a professional storyteller, and, because of your homework assignment, you will be especially interested in her workshop."

A new scene opened on a clear summer day in a park where four large tents had been erected. A large banner over the entrance to the biggest tent read, "Summer Solstice Storytellers Festival." At one of the smaller tents, a placard read, "Young Storytellers Workshop." Inside that smaller tent, a white-haired woman spoke to a group of kids.

"There is nothing quite like the thrill of telling a story to an audience," she said. "You hear them laugh at the funny parts, see them nervous at the scary parts, and know they are moved by the sentimental parts.

"I specialize in stories about my ancestors and stories my ancestors would have told. I've traced my genealogy back to western Africa, where storytelling was the job of certain families called griots. I like to think that I came from one of those families. But you can specialize in any type of story that interests you.

"Everybody likes a good story, and you can find so many opportunities to tell your stories. Sometimes you can create a

story out of your homework assignment and present it in front of your class, or maybe at a talent assembly. Libraries often hold mini festivals for stories. If you baby-sit, telling a good story can calm kids down at bedtime. Around the campfire is a wonderful place to tell stories. Sometimes there are opportunities at your church or religious center, or maybe there will be a program for a family reunion. And have you ever been stuck in a car for a long drive? Stories are a great way to make time fly for everyone in the car. Sleepover parties are natural places for storytelling. Of course, there are festivals like this one where you can perform. And once you get to be really good, you might be able to line up some professional gigs where you might actually get paid to tell stories!

"After you have made up your mind to become a storyteller, you need to come up with some stories that become your stories. I have three simple rules for you. First, find stories that you enjoy! If you like them, you can transfer your enthusiasm to your audience. Second, find stories that are appropriate for the audience or the event. A campfire story may not be good for church. Third, know how you want your audience to react, whether you want them to laugh and be entertained or be motivated to take some action.

"Now think of a good story you like, and we'll talk about how to make it a good storytelling story."

www.summerbridgeactivities.com **Reading Connection—Grade 6—RBP0210**

## Expanding Your Reading Power

1. Check the statements that are likely conclusions you can make about storytelling.

_____ Storytelling is for adults.

_____ Storytelling can only be done on a
stage.

_____ Storytelling is popular.

_____ Storytelling could be a handy skill
to develop.

2. Check the statement that is the best main
idea of this story.

_____ Librarians make good storytellers.

_____ Storytelling started in Africa.

_____ Some stories make people laugh.

_____ Kids can become storytellers.

3. Write a short summary about opportunities for storytelling.

_____

_____

_____

## Expanding Your Word Power

Write the words from this story that have the
meanings below.

1. when the sun is as far north or south as
possible _____

2. a poster _____

3. appealing to the emotions _____

4. a gathering of people who have been
separated _____

5. jobs for performers _____

6. great interest or excitement _____

7. Find the **idiom** in paragraph six and write
it. _____

8. Write the meaning of the idiom.

_____

_____

## Understanding Language

The word root **-audi-** relates to "hearing." Write
the letter of the word before its clue.

| a. audio | b. auditorium |
|----------|---------------|
| c. audible | d. audience |

1. _____ a place where an audience gathers

2. _____ loud enough to be heard

3. _____ people who hear and see a performance

4. _____ sound from a television or radio

## Expanding Other Skills

Complete this outline of paragraph 7.

I. Rules for finding stories.

A. _____

B. _____

C. _____

# How to Be a Successful Storyteller

Imagine yourself in front of an audience.

"Find a story that you like, one that will work for your audience. Then become part of the story and have the story become part of you. Usually that means that you make changes in the basic story. When you change a story, you are creating an adaptation.

"Sometimes it's fun to take a familiar story, like a folktale or legend, and change it to surprise your audience. Most people like stories that have twists and surprises.

"Sometimes it's fun to change some of the characters. You might make a wolf sympathetic instead of mean, for example.

"Sometimes it's fun to tell the story from a different point of view. For example, you could tell the story of Snow White from the point of view of the queen or the prince. Mark Twain did that when he put a modern character in King Arthur's court.

"Sometimes it's fun to put a familiar story in a different setting. The Cinderella story has Egyptian, Persian, and Korean versions.

"Maybe you would enjoy telling your story as one of the characters. You could be the wolf in 'Little Red Riding Hood.'

"When you write your script, look for words or phrases that can be repeated. Repeated words and phrases are very effective in stories told out loud. They are also a good way to get your audience involved. After a couple of times, you give the beginning of the repeated phrase and prompt the audience to say the rest of the phrase in unison. That's a form of call and response, as was used in the old African American spirituals. Repeated words and phrases also give rhythm to your story, and rhythm helps carry your audience with you.

"Visual aids add spice to your storytelling. Acting parts of the story adds excitement. Try using costumes and makeup, or even multiple costumes that you change as you tell the story. Try props, like different hats for different characters. Puppets are also good devices to catch people's interest.

"Music and sound effects add mood or sometimes humor to your story. Most griots in Africa accompany their stories with music. Music can also help you remember what comes next. For most people, it's easier to memorize a song with music than a poem without music.

"After you've developed your stories and your visual and sound aids, the next big step is to practice. Practice, practice, practice. Practice in front of a mirror. Practice in front of your pet. Practice in front of your family. Practice in front of friends who will encourage you. Taping your practice performance with a video camera helps tremendously. When you watch the tape, you will see which parts work best and which parts need improvement.

"Then comes the big payoff—your performance. Imagine the excitement inside as you step onto your stage and start your story. Imagine the great satisfaction of the rousing applause of an audience that loved what you did."

## Expanding Your Reading Power

1. Write an **S** before statements that describe only storytelling. Write an **A** before statements that describe only acting. Write **SA** before statements that describe both.

   _____ Shakespeare wrote mainly for this.

   _____ Performances can take place on stage.

   _____ It has been done for centuries.

   _____ It can be done with or without costumes.

2. Write **F** before each statement of fact. Write **O** before each statement of opinion.

   _____ Storytelling is not as important as other arts.

   _____ Storytelling is easiest with a small audience.

   _____ There are many versions of some stories.

   _____ Stories are better if told with props.

3. Number the order of the steps to becoming a successful storyteller.

   _____ Adapt the story for listening and props.

   _____ Find a story you and the audience will like.

   _____ Perform with enthusiasm.

   _____ Practice many times.

## Expanding Your Word Power

Write the words from this story that have the meanings below.

1. a story changed for some purpose _____ _____

2. to have compassion for _____

3. together _____

4. a regular beat _____

5. something used for a purpose, like a tool _____

6. exciting, spurring to action _____

**Homographs** are words that have the same spelling but different meanings. Write the **homographs** from the story that have meanings different than these definitions.

7. taking a break from work

   _____

8. a timepiece worn on a wrist

   _____

## Understanding Language

The word roots **-vid-** and **-vis-** mean "to see." Write the letter of the word before its clue.

| | |
|---|---|
| a. visage | b. invisible |
| c. videotape | d. video |

1. _____ cannot be seen

2. _____ the picture part of a television signal

3. _____ tape on which moving pictures may be recorded

4. _____ how something appears

## Expanding Other Skills

Check the information that is important in an advertisement for a storytelling performance.

_____ where the performer learned storytelling

_____ the place of the performance

_____ a record of past performances

_____ the date of the performance

_____ the time of the performance

_____ that it is a storytelling performance

# Philo's Great Vision

How do inventors start out?

"Okay," Ben said. "Stories don't have to be written, and you can find stories just about anywhere."

"Not just about anywhere," said Clio. "Everywhere! The basic building blocks of your universe are stories, not atoms."

"But science is science, not stories," Ben said.

Clio smiled wryly and waved in a new scene. A giant television materialized. It was as big as a movie theater screen. Huge gold letters across the top said "PhiloVision." An orchestra fanfare shook the ground. A log cabin appeared on the screen, and a deep, resonant voice, like a ship's horn, spoke.

"A remarkable scientist was born in this simple log cabin in Utah. The year was 1906. His name was Philo Taylor Farnsworth. His invention would change the world forever."

A slender, young boy with sandy hair and blue eyes turned through the pages of a Sears catalog. He looked in awe at the pictures of ringer washing tubs, wind-up clocks, radios, and electric motors. But the electric train sets were the best of all. Some families in town had these wonders. But his family didn't even have electricity.

"Six-year-old Philo told his family he was going to be an inventor. His heroes were Thomas Edison and Alexander Graham Bell. Going barefoot and wearing bib overalls, he went through the neighborhood gathering broken tools, wheel spokes, strands of loose wire, pieces of wood, and other discarded items. Then he set to work creating his own machines. He imagined he was making electric machines. None of them worked."

The narrator continued. "Ben, when Philo was your age, his family moved to a farm in Idaho.

"Their new home had electricity from an electric generator on the property. Philo was excited to have electricity for the first time. He loved to tinker and experiment with the generator. Sometimes his tinkering broke the generator. The repairman came often. Philo watched everything the repairman did. Before long, young Philo could fix the generator when it broke. His father was amazed by his 11-year-old son's ability with machines.

"Philo found a stack of science magazines in the attic. He studied them as often as he could. One idea in a magazine excited his imagination more than anything else. It was a prediction that someday motion pictures with sound would be sent over the airwaves the way sound was then sent to radios. The science writers called it television.

"Philo studied every book he could get on electricity, radio, broadcasting, and the idea of television. He decided that the inventors trying to create a working television were going about it all wrong. They used spinning mirrors or discs to capture the light of a scene. Motion picture cameras and sound recording machines started that way. Then the inventors changed the mechanical image to an electric signal that could go through wires or the air. Philo said that mechanical devices could never work fast enough for television."

Later, his calculations would prove it.

www.summerbridgeactivities.com
Reading Connection—Grade 6—RBP0210

## Expanding Your Reading Power

1. Check all the ways the reader of this story learns what Philo Farnsworth was like.

   _____ what Philo does

   _____ what Philo says

   _____ what Philo thinks

   _____ what other characters say and think about Philo

   _____ how the author directly describes Philo

2. List three things that helped Philo Farnsworth become an inventor.

   a. _____

   b. _____

   c. _____

3. Write what you predict will happen in the rest of this story.

   _____

   _____

## Expanding Your Word Power

Write the words from this story that have the meanings below.

1. crookedly _____

2. music used to draw attention

   _____

3. great respect touched with fear

   _____

4. no longer used _____

5. a machine that produces electricity

   _____

6. to experiment with machine parts

   _____

In each row below, circle the two words that are related.

7. mechanical     machine     month

8. tennis     band     orchestra

## Understanding Language

The prefix **tele-** means "operating from a distance" or "in, of, or by television." Match the words that have the prefix *tele-* with the meanings below.

| | | |
|---|---|---|
| a. telecast | b. teleconference | c. telecourse |
| d. television | e. telephone | f. telegraph |

1. _____ a class taken by television

2. _____ writing over distance

3. _____ television broadcast

4. _____ conference over distance

5. _____ hearing sound or voice over distance

6. _____ seeing over distance

## Expanding Other Skills

Check the words you might look up in a thesaurus to find synonyms for these words.

1. *cabin*

   _____ payment

   _____ habitation

   _____ disease

   _____ arms

2. *gold*

   _____ metal

   _____ fighting

   _____ smoothness

   _____ wisdom

3. *fanfare*

   _____ metal

   _____ explanation

   _____ religion

   _____ music

# Father of Television
How far would his invention go?

Philo T. Farnsworth knew that electrons were the key to making television work. Electrons are extremely small and fast. A stream of electrons can be bent into patterns. Those patterns can be sent through wires or through the air. Then a receiver can reassemble the picture from the pattern. Philo decided the electrons would need to capture 20 or 30 pictures every second. But he didn't know how to harness electrons to make pictures. He knew he could make television work if he could figure that out.

Fourteen-year-old Philo was working in the field on a beautiful spring day. He was guiding a three-horse team pulling a harrow to cut rows across a field. The work was tedious and potentially dangerous. It required concentration. Part of Philo's mind, however, was also working on his invention projects. He paused as he turned at the end of the field and looked back at the perfectly parallel rows in the dirt.

Suddenly an idea flashed in his mind. If a plot of earth could be divided into a series of lines, then why not a picture? The lines could be so small that the human eye would see the picture and not the lines. The electrons would create the rows super fast so that the images in the pictures would appear to be moving in steady motion.

His heart raced with excitement. He knew he had the answer he had been searching for. He knew how to make television work.

Philo worked on his idea in the months he was waiting to start high school. He was excited to get into a real science class. That fall, he talked his way into a senior chemistry class even though he was only a freshman. He shared his television ideas with his teacher after school one day. It took a few afternoons after school to explain everything to his astonished teacher. His teacher finally admitted that Philo's idea just might work.

Philo didn't finish college. Instead, he found investors to pay for his research when he was only 19 years old. A year later, in 1927, he applied for his first patents to protect his ideas. One year after that, he supervised the first successful electronic television transmission. Television was born, and Philo was the father.

Philo worked for years to refine his invention. After World War II, the government assigned airwaves for television. In 1946 there were 7,000 television sets in the United States. By 1950, there were 7,000,000. The boom was on.

Philo turned his attention to other inventions, but nothing for him topped his invention of television.

In 1969, Philo watched on his television as an astronaut walked on the moon. He was astonished to think that his idea had gone all the way from a farm field in Idaho to the surface of the moon.

Two years later, Philo Farnsworth contracted an illness and died. He was one of the great inventors and thinkers of the 20th century—and one man who changed the world.

www.summerbridgeactivities.com

## Expanding Your Reading Power

1. Why do you think Philo Farnsworth could be a successful inventor even though he was so young?

   _____

   _____

Write the words that best complete each sentence.

2. Her body got weak, and she _____ pneumonia.

   **contracted**     **greased**          **played**

3. He flunked the math test because of a lack of _____.

   toothbrush    concentration    karate

4. Check the statement that best describes how the plot of this story moves.

   _____ from problem to solution

   _____ from conflict to peace

   _____ from danger to safety

   _____ from dilemma to decision

## Expanding Your Word Power

Write the words from this story that have the meanings below.

1. to control the force of _____

2. a device to break up the ground

   _____

3. boringly slow or repetitious

   _____

4. government protection for an invention

   _____

5. a sent signal _____

6. Check the sentence in which *stream* has the same meaning as in paragraph 1.

   _____ Every afternoon, she went fishing in the stream.

   _____ He watched the stream of sunlight through the stained-glass window.

   _____ When the movie ends, the kids stream out.

## Understanding Language

The suffix **-ment** means "result or action." Match the words with *-ment* with the meanings.

| | |
|---|---|
| a. excitement | b. judgment |
| c. experiment | d. fulfillment |

1. _____ the action of testing

2. _____ the result of judging

3. _____ the state of feeling excited

4. _____ the result of being filled

## Expanding Other Skills

This chart shows the number of TVs for every 1,000 people. Use it to answer the questions.

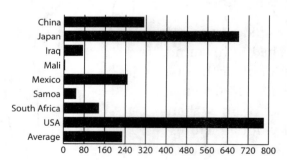

1. Which country has the most TVs?

   _____

2. Which country has the fewest TVs?

   _____

3. Which countries are below the average?

   _____

   _____

**Reading Connection—Grade 6—RBP0210**    www.summerbridgeactivities.com    ©**RBP Books**

# The Science behind the Magic of Television

Have you ever wondered how television works?

The music on the giant PhiloVision changed to a new fanfare, and Philo Farnsworth stepped out of the screen.

"Ben, I want to give you a quick tour of my invention."

Ben approached reluctantly. "Come on, you'll love this," Philo said, walking back into the screen. Ben stepped forward, and suddenly he was inside the television.

"All of this was created on one basic idea, as you heard, but we had a lot of problems to solve. Each time we came up with a solution, we took out a patent. I had patents for scanning, focusing, synchronizing, controlling, powering, and plenty of other stuff. But let's start your tour up here."

They walked to the smaller end of the tube to a metal device. "This is the cathode," Philo said. "When it heats up, it shoots out electrons, those particles that are in orbit around the nucleus of an atom. Those electrons go through this anode. The anode focuses the electrons into a narrow beam and accelerates their speed."

He pointed to copper wires coiled around the outside of the narrow end of the tube. "Those are the steering coils. They create magnetic pull on the beam of electrons to direct it across the screen."

They walked down into the bigger part of the tube with the flat end.

"The inside of this tube is a vacuum, so the electrons don't have to contend with the molecules of air. This flatter end of the tube is where the beam of electrons is aimed. This entire flat surface is coated with phosphor. A spot of phosphor glows when electrons strike it. A strong beam makes it glow white, no beam makes it stay black, and varying strengths produce shades of gray."

Philo waved his hand at the sides of the tube. "These sides have a special coating that conducts the electrons off the front to keep them from piling up. And that's the basics for inside a black and white television. Now I'll give you a demonstration in slow motion."

Electrons shot out of the cathode and were lined up into a beam in the anode. The beam looked like a wave with varying strengths of power. The beam hit the screen in the top left and moved horizontally to the right, painting the bits of phosphor into white and grays and black. Then the beam started again from the left, one row down, and again traveled to the right side.

"There are 525 rows on most screens," Philo said. "In regular speed, the beam paints each of those rows 30 times in each second. That's 15,750 lines in one second.

"Color television is similar, except that there are three beams of electrons and the screen is painted with pixels of red, green, and blue phosphors. Combinations of those three colors in different intensities can make all the colors you can see.

"So, that's my baby," Philo said with a huge grin.

## Expanding Your Reading Power

**1.** Number the events in the order they happen within a television.

_____ The heated cathode shoots out electrons.

_____ Electrons excite the phosphor to shades of white, grays, or colors.

_____ The steering coil directs a pattern of electrons to the screen.

_____ The anode focuses and accelerates electrons.

**2.** Check all the words that describe the tone of this story.

_____ sad

_____ imaginative

_____ informative

_____ scary

**3.** Write **T** before statements that are true. Write **F** before statements that are false.

_____ Steering coils create a magnetic pull on the electrons.

_____ Electrons are part of atoms.

_____ Electron beams hit the phosphor with a constant force.

_____ Color televisions use three electron beams.

## Expanding Your Word Power

Write the words from this story that have the meanings below.

**1.** with hesitation _____

**2.** core_____

**3.** the smallest unit of matter_____

**4.** a space empty of matter, including air

_____

**5.** small particles of atoms bound together

_____

**6.** small points that make up a bigger picture

_____

Write the words from the story that are **antonyms** (words that have the opposite meaning) for these words.

**7.** slows_____

**8.** submit _____

**9.** vertically _____

## Understanding Language

Rewrite each phrase below. Use possessive forms.

**1.** invention of Philo

_____

**2.** nucleus of an atom

_____

**3.** intensities of colors

_____

## Expanding Other Skills

Sometimes the endings of base words change when endings are added. Use a dictionary to write the spellings of the words below with **-ed** and **-ing** added.

|  | -ed | -ing |
|---|---|---|
| **1.** stop | _____ | _____ |
| **2.** scan | _____ | _____ |
| **3.** synchronize | _____ | _____ |
| **4.** vary | _____ | _____ |

# Your Mind Is Like a Television

What is the connection between your brain and your television?

"There is one more thing necessary to make television work," Philo Farnsworth told Ben. "The human brain. There are two principles of the brain that relate to the way television works.

"The first principle is this: if a picture is divided into patterns of small dots, the brain will reassemble those dots into a meaningful image. The brain will recognize what the divided image is a picture of. Machines, like computers, have an extremely difficult time doing this, but the human brain does it naturally. Photos printed in books, newspapers, and magazines are also printed as patterns of small dots.

"A second amazing principle of how the brain works is this: if an action scene is divided into a series of still pictures, and those pictures are shown rapidly in succession, the brain will see those still pictures as one moving picture. However, the minimum speed is 15 pictures per second. Fewer than that, and the scene will seem jerky. Television shows 30 pictures each second.

"So you see, the human brain is critical in making meaning from patterns. This happens in other ways beside television.

"When you hear a story, your ears are receiving sound waves of different frequencies. Your brain makes meaning out of sound waves it recognizes as words and then assembles the words into meaning in a story.

"And think about a printed story. It's just a bunch of black marks on paper. It takes someone to read those marks to bring the story to life. Only then, in the mind of the reader, does it become a story.

"Each person is like a television system. Like television cameras, people focus their attention and take in signals. Then, like television sets, they assemble those signals into patterns that make meaning in their brains. These meanings are the stories that make up their personal universe, which is different for each person.

"It's like the old story from India of the blind men and the elephant.

"Six blind men were brought to an elephant by a wise man. He asked them for their opinion about an elephant. The first man felt only the trunk. 'It is like a large snake,' he said. The second man felt the elephant's side. 'An elephant,' he said, 'is like a wall.' The third man felt only the elephant's ear. 'An elephant is neither a snake nor a wall,' he said, 'but a fan.' The fourth man grabbed the elephant's leg. 'You are all wrong,' he said. 'An elephant is a tree.' The fifth man took hold of the smooth, pointed tusk and said, 'An elephant is a spear.' Then the last man grabbed the tail and declared that the elephant is really a rope.

"Each man spoke truthfully about what he perceived, yet each man was wrong by assuming he had the whole meaning of the elephant.

"We are like the blind men. Each of us takes in part of the information around us to become part of our own story. Only when we share our stories with each other do we begin to uderstand the bigger picture of life."

www.summerbridgeactivities.com **Reading Connection—Grade 6—RBP0210**

## Expanding Your Reading Power

1. Write **B** before statements that are true only of the brain. Write **T** before statements that are true only of television. Write **BT** before statements that are true of both.

   _____ turns patterns of signals into meaning

   _____ can recognize patterns of pixels as a picture

   _____ can select the signals to receive

   _____ can be replaced without much difficulty

2. Check the statement that is the best main idea for this story.

   _____ Similarities exist in how televisions and brains work.

   _____ Human brains can make assumptions.

   _____ It took human brains to invent television.

   _____ Blind men don't know what an elephant really is.

3. Check the most likely conclusions about the human brain.

   _____ The brain processes a lot of information.

   _____ The brain is never wrong in how it perceives things.

   _____ The brain requires sight to function well.

   _____ Stories are part of how the brain makes meaning.

## Expanding Your Word Power

Write the words from this story that have the meanings below.

1. one after another _____

2. extremely important _____

3. repetitions within a time span

   _____

4. supposing _____

5. taken in through the senses _____

Write **M** before phrases that are metaphors. Write **S** before phrases that are similes.

6. _____ An elephant is like a wall.

7. _____ An elephant is a tree.

8. _____ The elephant is really a rope.

## Understanding Language

Write the **compound words** from the story that are formed by adding to these base words.

1. paper _____

2. one _____

## Expanding Other Skills

Complete this partial outline of paragraph 9.

  II. First blind man

    A. feels only the elephant's trunk

    B. says elephant is like a large snake

  III. Second blind man

    A. _____

    B. _____

  IV. _____

    A. _____

    B. _____

  V. _____

    A. _____

    B. _____

# Keeping a Journal

How can a journal help you?

The scene of Philo and the giant PhiloVision broke into horizontal lines and faded away. A new scene opened up and Ben found himself inside a large bookstore, standing in a crowd of people. Many of the people held copies of a book, and on the back cover of the book was a photo of the author, who was standing in front of them, talking to them through a microphone.

"Each of us has one main story," the writer said. "That story is the story of our life. But that one big story is made up of a lot of other little stories. Those little stories are what happens to us day by day and how we respond.

"So ask yourself, what are you going to do with the stories of your life?" The writer looked straight into Ben's eyes and smiled.

"I record those stories in my journal," the author went on. "Whether or not you aspire to a career in writing, keeping a journal can be a very powerful tool in your life. I have seven rules for empowering your life through journal writing. Here they are in reverse order.

"Number seven—use writing to record happy times and good things that happen to you. When you feel sad or upset, rereading what you wrote at happier times can lift your spirits.

"Number six—use writing in your journal to help you solve problems. Sometimes we talk about our problems with our friends or family. Other times we need to work through our problems by ourselves, and writing about them is probably the best way to do that. In that way, your journal can be your silent friend. Often problems seem simpler when they are written down on paper, and they stop circling around in your mind. Also, when you write, you open yourself up to inspiration on how to deal with issues.

"Number five—use writing in your journal to help you discover things about yourself, your thoughts, and your feelings. You will often surprise yourself once you start writing. Write about any subject that interests you. Your writing will be a record of your exploration and discovery, and it can help open up exciting ideas that wouldn't come to you without writing.

"Number four—use writing to clarify your goals and organize your activities. Writing your goals and plans helps to make them happen.

"Number three—write down ideas right when they come, even in the middle of the night. If you don't, they'll slip away and be gone forever. Then transfer your idea notes to your journal.

"Number two—write frequently in your journal. Some people write in their journals every day, and that's great. But, if you can't write every day, write often. Make writing in your journal a strong habit.

"And the number one rule—if you aren't already keeping a journal, start today!"

www.summerbridgeactivities.com    **Reading Connection—Grade 6—RBP0210**

## Expanding Your Reading Power

1. Check the most likely reason the author had for writing this story.

   _____ to entertain readers with jokes

   _____ to motivate readers to keep a journal

   _____ to present facts without embellishment

   _____ to sell products

Circle the word that best completes each sentence.

2. He wanted to _____ the story to reinforce his understanding.

   **reread**          **forget**          **avoid**

3. New ideas and _____ often came to her in the shower.

   **errors**          **honors**          **inspiration**

## Expanding Your Word Power

Write the words from this story that have the meanings below.

1. strive toward a goal _____

2. life's work _____

3. to make clear _____

4. established pattern of behavior

   _____

5. Check the sentence in which *broke* has the same meaning as in paragraph 1.

   _____ The cushions broke his fall.

   _____ The tape got stuck when the VCR broke.

   _____ They couldn't buy the car because they were broke.

   _____ The vase fell and broke into dozens of pieces.

6. Check the sentence in which *record* has the same meaning as in paragraph 5.

   _____ It was the coldest day on record.

   _____ Don't forget to record your progress as you go.

   _____ She found an old phonograph and a record in the attic.

   _____ He held the school record for the 100-meter dash.

## Understanding Language

The prefix **trans-** means "across or beyond." Match the words that have the prefix **trans-** with the meanings below.

| a. transfer | b. transmit | c. transplant |
| d. transport | e. transcribe | |

1. _____ to uproot and replant

2. _____ to write out fully, from notes

3. _____ to change from one person or place to another

4. _____ to send a signal

5. _____ to carry from one place to another

## Expanding Other Skills

Complete this partial outline. (Do not put the ideas in reverse order as they are in the story.)

I. How to empower your life with journal writing.

   A. Start writing a journal today!

   B. _____

   C. _____

   D. _____

   E. _____

   F. _____

   G. _____

# Reaching an Audience
Where can you publish your writing?

The people in the crowd applauded vigorously. The author smiled and nodded at them in appreciation, then handed the microphone to a woman.

"On behalf of our store, I want to thank all of you for being here," she said. "After a brief break, we'll proceed to the book autographing at this table."

The author walked toward Ben, pausing briefly to shake people's hands, and then put out his hand for Ben to shake.

"Ben, come with me. We need to talk." Ben followed the author away from the crowd.

"You're having a debate with yourself, and part of you thinks you could be a writer."

"How do you know?" Ben asked.

"I know," the author said. "And I know that you can become a successful professional writer and that it will be easier if you start working toward that goal right now."

"But I'm still kind of young," Ben said.

The writer took a book from a shelf and opened it. Instead of words, Ben saw a moving scene of a young girl with short, black hair, about his age, wearing clothes from more than 50 years earlier. She sat in a small room writing.

"That's Anne Frank," the writer said. "Even though she was just your age, she's touched the lives of millions of people because she took the time to write down some of the stories from her short life."

The writer opened another book, and another moving scene jumped into Ben's view. It was another girl Ben's age from a more recent time. Again, this girl was writing. "That's Zlata Filipovic, a young girl in what used to be Yugoslavia. She started keeping a journal, and then war came to her city of Sarajevo. She wrote about how the war affected her and her family. Her journal was published, and because of that she has been able to raise money to help other children orphaned or displaced by war.

"And why did their writing touch people? One reason is that they wrote from the heart, and readers connect to that. Imagine how gratifying it is to have people you have never met come up to you with honest enthusiasm and tell you how much what you wrote meant to them. That's a fantastic reward!

"As a writer I work hard, but I can work wherever I want, and on my schedule. And as the writer Emerson said, 'There are no days in life so memorable as those which vibrated to some stroke of the imagination.'

"As an adolescent, you should write for yourself, but you can also write for others. Young people today have so many opportunities to publish their writing—school publications, magazines especially for youth writing, books of youth writing, and many sites on the Internet. Or you can set up your own web site. New printing technologies make self-publishing very feasible.

"All it takes is a little research, a healthy dose of determination, and, of course, some good writing."

## Expanding Your Reading Power

1. Check the words that best describe the author in this story.

   _____ famous

   _____ tense

   _____ encouraging

   _____ trickster

2. Write **F** before each statement of fact. Write **O** before each statement of opinion.

   _____ Millions of people know Anne Frank's story.

   _____ Anne's diary is better than Zlata's diary.

   _____ Only teenagers enjoy writing by teenagers.

   _____ There are many ways for teenagers to get their writing published.

3. Write a short summary about opportunities young people have to be published.

   _____

   _____

   _____

## Expanding Your Word Power

Write the words from this story that have the meanings below.

1. energetically _____

2. move on to or continue with

   _____

3. removed from a place _____

4. very pleasing _____

5. capable of being accomplished; possible

   _____

6. Find the **idiom** in paragraph 11 and write it. _____

7. Explain what the idiom means. _____

   _____

## Understanding Language

Rewrite each phrase below. Use possessive forms.

1. hands of the people _____

   _____

2. work of the writer _____

   _____

3. works of the writers _____

   _____

## Expanding Other Skills

A **bibliography** contains a list of articles or books that an author used for reference when writing. Read these entries in a bibliography. Then answer the questions.

---

A. **Covington, Richard.** "Forever Young." *Smithsonian* Oct. 2001: 70.

B. **Filipovic, Zlata.** *Zlata's Diary: A Child's Life in Sarajevo.* New York: Viking, 1994.

C. **Frank, Anne.** *Anne Frank, the Diary of a Young Girl.* New York: Modern Library, 1952.

---

1. Check the information given in entry A for a magazine article.

   ____ author         ____ page number

   ____ publisher      ____ date of magazine

   ____ article title  ____ name of magazine

2. Check the information given in entries B and C for books.

   ____ author         ____ page number

   ____ publisher      ____ date of publication

   ____ book title     ____ city of publication

# Where Do You Get Your Ideas?

How do you encourage inspiration?

Ben thought back to the time in his bedroom before he had been swept away to Fabulaterra. He had been determined to write the best story he could possibly write. He had sat with paper and pencil, and then at the computer, but the story wouldn't come.

"I want to write," Ben said, "but where do you get your ideas for your stories?"

The author smiled as if he had been anticipating that question. He reached to the top shelf for a big book titled *Mythology* and took it down. "In ancient Greece, Zeus was called the father of the gods of Olympus. Zeus had children whose mother was Mnemosyne, the Titaness of memory."

He opened the book, and Ben saw teenaged girls dressed in wispy tunics singing, dancing, and playing musical instruments in a bright, sunny meadow.

"The nine daughters of Zeus and Mnemosyne are called the Muses. The Greeks claimed they inspired poets, writers, musicians, dancers, actors, scientists, or anyone else doing creative work. Our words *music*, *museum*, and *amusement* come from the word *muse*."

He turned the pages, showing Ben each of the beautiful young women. "This one is my special friend," he said. The girl in the picture had her back to them, but when she turned and smiled at Ben, he was shocked. It was Clio.

The author gently closed the book, replaced it, and took down another. "Creative people use different methods to encourage ideas, or, as many say, to entice their Muse to help them."

He opened the book, and each time he turned a page a different person gave Ben advice for getting ideas to come.

"Muses aren't interested in people who aren't actively working on a project. You can't get your Muse to come to you if you're just wasting your time with frivolous pastimes. If you're a writer, get writing, even if it's a struggle at first. After enough effort, you'll find your Muse helping you with ideas that pop into your head.

"The ancient Greeks made offerings to the Muses. One of your offerings is experience. Record your experiences in your journal and look for the meanings in them. Be a careful observer of everything around you. Read every day. Reading gives you vicarious experience. Read different genres.

"Don't ignore your Muse, or she'll leave you. When you get an idea, use it right away. Then more ideas will come.

"Let your mind work on getting ideas while you are doing other things, like harrowing a field, doing the dishes, riding a bicycle, or even playing video games.

"Create playful daydreams around your project. If you do this at night when you go to bed, often your mind will search for new ideas as you sleep."

The author closed the book. "Ben," he said, "you can't force an idea, and you can't control creativity. All you can do is go through your creative process and then be open and ready when the ideas come."

## Expanding Your Reading Power

1. Write a brief summary about muses from the information in paragraphs 3–6.

   _____

   _____

   _____

2. List five ways to help ideas come.

   a. _____

   b. _____

   c. _____

   d. _____

   e. _____

3. The author talks about the process of being creative. What helps you be creative?

   _____

   _____

   _____

## Expanding Your Word Power

Write the words from this story that have the meanings below.

1. waiting for _____

2. loose-fitting garment _____

3. not serious _____

4. not actual, but in the imagination

   _____

5. categories of literature _____

6. a system to produce something

   _____

In each row below, circle the two words related to the word in bold type.

7. **wispy**

   filmy            thin            obese

8. **offerings**

   lies            gifts            sacrifices

## Understanding Language

*Muse* has become the base word for other words. Write the letter of the word before its clue.

| a. muse | b. music | c. museum |
|---|---|---|
| d. amuse | e. amusement | |

1. _____ Temple of the Muses, with inspired art and ideas

2. _____ to entertain (originally meant "to be inspired by a muse")

3. _____ an entertainment

4. _____ to ponder or meditate

5. _____ Muse-inspired sound

## Expanding Other Skills

Complete this recipe by adding the items below.

hard work    goal setting    reading often
actual experience    vicarious experience
purposeful daydreaming    journal writing

Recipe for
Creative Process Stew

2 parts_____    4 parts_____
1 part _____    2 parts_____
3 parts_____    1 part _____
3 parts_____

Directions:

First, mix _____ with _____. Then, blend in _____, _____, and _____. Add _____ and _____ to taste. Cook for _____ (time), stirring often. Serve to your guests, and enjoy!

"Could I interrupt briefly?" a woman asked the author. "Your books mean so much to me. I want to thank you and ask if you would autograph this copy for me because I have to leave."

"I'd be delighted to in just a moment." The author turned to Ben and said, "Ben, start now to develop a good writer's habits. Your future starts now." Then he handed a book to Ben, turned back to the woman, and walked to the table where he autographed her book. People lined up waiting to have their copies of the author's book signed. He smiled and talked amiably with each person as he wrote inside the books. As the scene started to fade, the author looked up at Ben and smiled one last time before the bookstore disappeared.

Ben looked around for Clio, but she was not there. He almost panicked, wondering if he would be stuck forever in Fabulaterra.

"Clio?" he called. But there was no answer.

He sat down in the grass, and the memories of all that had happened in Fabulaterra flooded his mind. He saw the orc and Clio tied near the tree. He saw Tolkien and Bilbo and thought how Tolkien had fed his imagination with the legends of Odin, Thor, and other heroes. He saw Gandhi learning the Hindu stories and guiding his people to freedom. He saw Martin Luther King Jr. inspiring people with big words and big ideas. He saw storytellers. He saw young Philo Farnsworth getting his spark of inspiration as he harrowed a field.

"The power for creativity comes from work *and* inspiration," he mused to himself. "And every meaning is a story built on stories."

He glanced down at the book the author had placed in his hands. It hadn't faded with the rest of the scene. He opened it and read, "Joseph was 11 when his father got sick." He turned the page and saw a moving picture of his great-great-grandfather, Joseph, who had been 11 when his father died. He had become the man of the family and helped his mother move west to create a new home in the wilderness. He saw Joseph and his mother, Martha Ann, standing on the crest of a hill, looking west. The sun rising behind their backs cast long shadows stretching out far in front of them.

A jolt of excitement ran through Ben. He knew the whole story he would write, and he knew it would be good.

"You're ready to go back," Clio said, suddenly standing beside Ben.

Ben nodded. "I'm ready, but before I go, tell me who that author was."

Clio grinned. "That's you, Ben, 20 years from now, if you live for it."

In an instant Ben found himself back in his own room, seated at the computer. He switched off the video game, turned on the word processing program, whispered, "Thank you, Clio," and started typing: "Joseph was 11 when his father got sick."

## Expanding Your Reading Power

1. Check the likely conclusions from the story.

   _____ We can have a variety of experiences through stories.

   _____ Stories affect us more than we often realize.

   _____ Ideas come only from a muse.

   _____ Ideas usually come when we follow a creative process.

2. In most stories, the main characters are changed by what they experience. Number the events in the order they happened.

   _____ Ben is transported to Fabulaterra.

   _____ Ben understands stories and the creative process.

   _____ Ben gets an idea and uses it to start writing his story.

   _____ Ben experiences many stories, guided by Clio, the Muse.

   _____ Ben determines to write a good story but is frustrated.

3. Write what you think will happen to Ben with this assignment. How will his teacher and classmates react?

   _____

   _____

   _____

## Expanding Your Word Power

Write the words from this story that have the meanings below.

1. in a friendly way _____

2. overpowered by terror _____

3. thought about or reflected _____

4. the top of something _____

5. to project _____

Write the words from the story that are **homophones** (words with the same sound but different spellings and meanings) for these words.

6. rote _____

7. steak _____

Write the words from the story that are **homographs** (words with the same spelling but different meanings) for these definitions.

8. nasty, not nice _____

9. plaster case for a broken limb _____

## Understanding Language

The word root -**voc**- means "call." Write the letter of the word before its clue.

| | |
|---|---|
| a. vocabulary | b. vocation |
| c. vocalist | d . vocal |

1. _____ inclined to speak freely

2. _____ a career

3. _____ a list of words

4. _____ a singer

## Expanding Other Skills

Write the letters of the reference materials you might use to lead you to more information on the subjects listed below.

| | |
|---|---|
| a. encyclopedia | b. atlas |
| c. dictionary | d. almanac |
| e. library card catalog | f. internet |
| g. newspaper | |

1. _____ myths and legends

2. _____ how to spark creativity

3. _____ meaning of the prefix *hyper-*

4. _____ maps of where Gandhi lived

## Page 6

### Expanding Your Reading Power

1. goal setter
2. Ben wants to win the respect of the teacher and other students.
3. Ben finds himself in a fantasy world.

### Expanding Your Word Power

1. subtle
2. ancestors
3. immigrating
4. captivating
5. envision
6. intensified
7. Nixon had been President when his mother was a kid.
8. Alex whipped around the corner.

### Understanding Language

1. clearly
2. patiently
3. seriously
4. blankly
5. suddenly

### Expanding Other Skills

1. Ireland   A
2. Italy   E
3. Denmark   B
4. Germany   C
5. Spain   D

## Page 8

### Expanding Your Reading Power

1. tense
2. football
3. He had practiced virtual sword fighting (in video games).
4. fantasy

### Expanding Your Word Power

1. bared
2. parry
3. stench
4. peculiar
5. desperation
6. momentum
7. gleaming
8. They were moving around each other.
9. He was trying to stop breathing so hard and fast.

### Understanding Language

1. disbelief
2. disagreeable
3. disadvantage
4. disappear
5. distrustful

### Expanding Other Skills

1. agile
2. bare
3. campfire
4. cautious
5. momentum
6. parry

## Page 10

### Expanding Your Reading Power

1. to entertain
2. caring
3. A person can go many places in his or her imagination.
4. Clio will help Ben learn to use his imagination in his writing.

### Expanding Your Word Power

1. reassured
2. lilted
3. delicate
4. jolt
5. eager
6. evolved
7. spectacles
8–9. Answers will vary.

### Understanding Language

1. reassured
2. retreat
3. lightly
4. slowly
5. instantly

### Expanding Other Skills

1. evolve
2. animé
3. enchant
4. aura

## Page 12

### Expanding Your Reading Power

1. upset about the evils of war
2. F, O, O, F
3. 3, 1, 4, 2
4. Answers will vary.

### Expanding Your Word Power

1. intrigued
2. aptitude
3. enlisted
4. portrayed
5. transferred
6. absent-mindedly
7. power
8. intelligence
9. invent
10. England
11. Tea Club Barrovian Society
12. World War One

### Understanding Language

1. conducting
2. education

### Expanding Other Skills

1. 52°, 30 min. latitude & 2° longitude
2. southwest

© RBP Books     www.summerbridgeactivities.com     Reading Connection—Grade 6—RBP0210

## Page 14

### Expanding Your Reading Power
1. To introduce readers to Tolkien's book *The Hobbit*.
2. H, HB, H, H & HB
3. Bilbo returned home after a successful adventure.

### Expanding Your Word Power
1. entranced
2. trilogy
3. startled
4. extending
5. involved
6. respectable
7. lair
8. survive
9. quickly
10. darkness

### Understanding Language
1. good-natured
2. hair-covered
3. two-handed

### Expanding Other Skills
A1. Shire
2. Bag-End

B1. trolls
2. elves, Rivendale
3. orcs, wargs
4. eagles
5. ring
6. Gollum
7. spiders
8. barrel
9. Smaug/a dragon

## Page 16

### Expanding Your Reading Power
1. Answers will vary.
2. compassionate
3. competitive
4. Agnar will be lost at sea. Geirrod will become king.

### Expanding Your Word Power
1. fertile
2. nourish
3. bleak
4. leaden
5. dinghy
6. observant
7. brash
8. boisterous
9. chasm
10. probing
11. author, novelist
12. shack, shanty
13. tales, dramas

### Understanding Language
1. fisherman
2. rainbow
3. birthright

### Expanding Other Skills
1. 0
2. Dec., Jan., Feb., Mar.
3. April

## Page 18

### Expanding Your Reading Power
1. concerned
2. F, F, T, T
3. fate
4. Knowledge and wisdom are extremely valuable.

### Expanding Your Word Power
1. forebodings
2. apprehensions
3. verified
4. overseer
5. hesitation
6. plucked
7. "which way the wind blows"

### Understanding Language
1. apprehensions
2. hesitation
3. finally
4. immediately

### Expanding Other Skills
1. d.
2. f.
3. a.
4. b.
5. e.
6. c.

## Page 20

### Expanding Your Reading Power
1. tense
2. A. He was a leader of thieves.
   B. Odin sings about a prince whose followers are criminals.
3. Answers will vary.
4. what Geirrod does/what Geirrod says/ what other characters say about him

### Expanding Your Word Power
1. furiously
2. reined in
3. gruffly
4. uncouth
5. despot
6. ambitious
7. trained
8. rules
9. fool
10. warmth

### Understanding Language
1. King Hrauding's house
2. servant's disguise
3. king's hospitality
4. whereabouts
5. leftover

### Expanding Other Skills
1. You use the ingredients in the same order they are listed on the recipe.
2. Answers will vary.

## Page 22

### Expanding Your Reading Power
1. GA, A, G, A
2. Criminals will pay for their crimes.
3. 1, 4, 6, 2, 3, 5, 8, 7
4. Answers will vary.

### Expanding Your Word Power
1. consumed
2. plunder
3. unscathed
4. hospitality
5. commotion
6. henchmen
7. heir
8. ate like wolves
9. Answers will vary.

### Understanding Language
1. unscathed
2. unharmed
3. furious
4. victorious

### Expanding Other Skills
1. dictionary
2. atlas
3. a book of myths
4. encyclopedia
5. almanac

## Page 24

### Expanding Your Reading Power
1. O, O, F, F
2. Wisdom is a valuable treasure.
3. 4, 1, 2, 3

### Expanding Your Word Power
1. integrity
2. compassion
3. unsurpassed
4. profound
5. elaborate
6. elevating
7. distraught
8. clear as glass
9. Answers will vary.

### Understanding Language
1. goodness
2. kindness
3. falseness

### Expanding Other Skills
1. d
2. e
3. b
4. f
5. a
6. c
7. nutmeg, cinnamon, clove

## Page 26

### Expanding Your Reading Power
1. He learned it from the dwarves' songs.
2. DG, G, D, D
3. consequence

### Expanding Your Word Power
1. consequences
2. gleefully
3. capsized
4. millstone
5. torment
6. wailed
7. caverns
8. fed
9. asleep
10. scooped
11. filled

### Understanding Language
1. giants'
2. husbands'
3. songs'
4. sons'

### Expanding Other Skills
1. a buddy
2. the shallow end
3. flotation devices
4. gum or food

## Page 28

### Expanding Your Reading Power
1. He loved his treasure more than his daughter.
2. a. He had a magic whetstone.
   b. He did the work of nine men.
3. Answers will vary.

### Expanding Your Word Power
1. valuable
2. enchanted
3. frightful
4. scythe
5. whetstone
6. gracious
7. Where will you hide your Easter eggs?
8. His favorite sandwich was made with seven-grain bread.
9. Winter can be a harsh, long season in Alaska.

### Understanding Language
1. giants' land
2. Mimir's well's water
3. Suttung's home
4. nine men's work
5. the season's work

### Expanding Other Skills
1. val-u-a-ble/valu-able
2. own-er-ship
3. hos-pi-tal-i-ty
4. wan-der-er

## Page 30

### Expanding Your Reading Power
1. to entertain
2. ashamed, hopeless
3. diminish
4. 1, 3, 2, 5, 4, 6

### Expanding Your Word Power
1. diminish
2. auger
3. bore
4. penetrated
5. gnarled
6. reversed
7. dispense
8. vault, room
9. cape, coat

### Understanding Language
1. not polite
2. not possible
3. not patient
4. not mobile
5. not movable
6. not pure

### Expanding Other Skills
a, b, d, c

## Page 32

### Expanding Your Reading Power
1. Answers will vary.
2. mighty
3. O, F, O, F
4. Loki discovers that the giants stole the hammer.

### Expanding Your Word Power
1. massive
2. vow
3. dangled
4. elegant
5. priceless
6. depriving
7. cunning
8. malicious
9. protect
10. connected
11. tricks

### Understanding Language
1. malicious
2. bad nutrition; not nourishing
3. hammer's magic
4. Miolnir's booming crash
5. Asgard's protector
6. Valkyries' queen

### Expanding Other Skills
A. 1. hammer
   2. belt
   3. glove
B. 1. feather cape

## Page 34

### Expanding Your Reading Power
1. humorous
2. F, O, O, F
3. He is good at fooling others.
4. Thor gets his hammer back.

### Expanding Your Word Power
1. grooming
2. league
3. recompense
4. covet
5. barter
6. relent
7. stifle
8. embroidery
9. nearby
10. thick

### Understanding Language
1. witless
2. hopeless
3. unable to help
4. without doubt
5. still; without motion

### Expanding Other Skills
1. 1. book about historical costumes
   2. encyclopedia
2. a. Internet (answers will vary)
   b. encyclopedia (answers will vary)

## Page 36

### Expanding Your Reading Power
1. self-centered
2. person vs. person
3. 4, 1, 5, 7, 2, 6, 3
4. Answers will vary.

### Expanding Your Word Power
1. hoarse
2. conceited
3. ravenously
4. devour
5. oaf
6. garments
7. uproariously
8. ahead
9. horse
10. poor

### Understanding Language
1. suspiciously
2. ravenously
3. uproariously

### Expanding Other Skills
1. sought
2. hoarse
3. fiery
4. oaf

## Page 38

### Expanding Your Reading Power
1. Don't let things that matter less keep you from things that matter more.
2. She is not mortal.
3. She wants to help people make good stories.

### Expanding Your Word Power
1. salivate
2. revelers
3. subside
4. awesome
5. potential
6. achieve
7. great
8. son
9. whether
10. scene

### Understanding Language
1. salivate
2. uncomfortable
3. awesome
4. potential

### Expanding Other Skills
1. desire, hunger
2. fasting, satisfaction

## Page 40

### Expanding Your Reading Power
1. 5, 3, 1, 2, 4
2. sapphire
3. Yudhistira will attempt to answer the questions before drinking.

### Expanding Your Word Power
1. stalking
2. fatigued
3. verdant
4. quench
5. serene
6. lament
7. heart dropped: to become sad or discouraged

### Understanding Language
1. too old
2. cloudy
3. coat worn over clothes
4. to eat too much
5. to miss or not see
6. across the ocean

### Expanding Other Skills
1. D
2. G
3. C
4. F
5. E
6. A
7. B

## Page 42

### Expanding Your Reading Power
1. to teach principles of good Hindu behavior
2. G, B, G, G
3. brave, humble

### Expanding Your Word Power
1. mystified
2. rites
3. vanquished
4. homage
5. parched
6. revived
7. help, love
8. obligation, responsiblity

### Understanding Language
1. not colored
2. agreeable
3. readable

### Expanding Other Skills
1. D, E, B, C, A, F

## Page 44

### Expanding Your Reading Power
1. Sometimes mind power is more important than physical power.
2. fable
3. The rabbit king tricks the elephants into leaving the rabbits' pool.

### Expanding Your Word Power
1. obvious
2. predicament
3. dregs
4. trumpeted
5. ripples
6. reflection
7. surrounding
8. quenching

### Understanding Language
1. footsteps
2. elephant-sized
3. rabbits' king
4. moon's reflection
5. Moon God's messenger
6. rabbits' lives

### Expanding Other Skills
1. almanac
2. atlas
3. a book of fables
4. encyclopedia
5. dictionary

# Answer Pages

## Page 46

### Expanding Your Reading Power
1. determined, well-educated
2. O, F, F, O
3. Answers will vary. He helped the country win its independence or helped to establish the country.

### Expanding Your Word Power
1. tolerance
2. solace
3. frail
4. client
5. restricting
6. principles
7. prime minister
8. University of Bombay
9. University College in London
10. Supreme Court of South Africa

### Understanding Language
1. connection
2. population
3. discrimination
4. the story of a life
5. your signature
6. "writing" made by light
7. study of the earth

### Expanding Other Skills
1. 12 Oct. 1893
2. M.K. Gandhi
3. Johannesburg
4. First class
5. 32 hours, 12 minutes

## Page 48

### Expanding Your Reading Power
1. 2, 1, 3, 4
2. All are checked.
3. Answers will vary.
4. Answers will vary.

### Expanding Your Word Power
1. pamphlet
2. discrimination
3. loom
4. caste
5. hostilities
6. prohibit
7. boycott

### Understanding Language
1. injustices
2. evaporated
3. independence
4. homeland
5. loincloth
6. seawater
7. freedom
8. to make free

### Expanding Other Skills
1. a small house
2. a small bed
3. a teacher or expert
4. a force related to consequences of actions
5. to wash your hair

## Page 50

### Expanding Your Reading Power
1. Preserving stories was important even when there was no written language.
2. WO, W, O, O
3. Answers will vary.

### Expanding Your Word Power
1. obituary
2. exploits
3. crucially
4. nutured
5. apprentices
6. weak
7. passed
8. bare

### Understanding Language
1. skin that is brown
2. with legs crossed
3. like a skirt
4. a study of family history
5. the origins or cause of something
6. true, real

### Expanding Other Skills
1. West Africa
2. West Africa

## Page 52

### Expanding Your Reading Power
1. to entertain
2. selfish, sneaky
3. humorous
4. myth

### Expanding Your Word Power
1. splendid
2. trickster
3. dangling
4. frustration
5. scattered
6. exchange
7. She wanted to hear the rest of the story.
8. She expected him to have a fit when she said, "No."

### Understanding Language
1. d
2. a
3. f
4. c
5. e
6. b

### Expanding Other Skills
1. c
2. e
3. b
4. a
5. d

## Page 54

### Expanding Your Reading Power
1. Mmoboro trusted Anansi.
   Anansi had devised a good plan.
2. F, T, F, T
3. Anansi will capture Onini and take him to Nyame.

### Expanding Your Word Power
1. fearsome    2. devise
3. gourds    4. drenched
5. soaking    6. wad
7. knives for claws
8. spear points for teeth

### Understanding Language
1. foolish—having qualities of a fool
2. somewhat green
3. preoccupied with oneself
4. embarrassed
5. full of mischief

### Expanding Other Skills
A. 1. hornets
    2. terrible sting
B. 1. python
    2. swallows men whole
C. 1. leopard
    2. knives for claws
    3. spear points for teeth

## Page 56

### Expanding Your Reading Power
1. OS, M, O, M
2. Clever solutions to problems can be entertaining.
   The stories are fun ways to teach morals.
3. Anansi tricks and captures Mmoboro, Onini, and Osebo. He takes them to the sky god and receives the stories.

### Expanding Your Word Power
1. slithered    2. prowled
3. sapling    4. yanking
5. dizzy    6. bind
7. sturdy, solid    8. python, reptile

### Understanding Language
1. asleep    2. aboard
3. afoot    4. around

### Expanding Other Skills
1. animal    2. plant, tree
3. complaint, drama

## Page 58

### Expanding Your Reading Power
1. sneaky, clever
2. O, F, O, O
3. 1, 4, 2, 3

### Expanding Your Word Power
1. sly    2. okra
3. pleaded    4. gunnysack
5. flustered
6. He cut a long, thin willow switch.

### Understanding Language
1. grandmother's story
2. fence's gate
3. one who plays tricks
4. someone old
5. someone young

### Expanding Other Skills
1. Modern. Answers will vary.
2. Answers will vary.

## Page 60

### Expanding Your Reading Power
1. Some slave songs had hidden meanings.
2. the Underground Railroad
3. the dividing line, especially rivers, between the North and the South
4. people who helped slaves escape
5. the free states

### Expanding Your Word Power
1. morphed    2. resonant
3. underground    4. plantation
5. bloodhounds    6. chariot
7. passion    8. memorize

### Understanding Language
1. underground    2. railroad
3. bloodhound

### Expanding Other Skills
1. the Ohio River, the Missouri River
2. approximately 200 miles (answers will vary between 150 and 225)

## Page 62

### Expanding Your Reading Power
1. brave, educated, determined
2. Answers will vary.
   a. the writings of Gandhi
   b. his father's preaching
   c. his mother, the unfairness of the laws
3. T, T, F, F

### Expanding Your Word Power
1. emancipation
2. proclamation
3. doctorate
4. boycott
5. mall
6. jail
7. trips

### Understanding Language
1. faraway
2. not violent
3. not for profit
4. making no sense
5. factual, not fiction
6. without stopping

### Expanding Other Skills
1. a. Answers will vary.
   b. Answers will vary.
2. a. Answers will vary.
   b. Answers will vary.

## Page 64

### Expanding Your Reading Power
1. to help people understand changes that needed to be made
   to encourage people who were working for civil rights
2. transformed
3. oppression
4. passionate, motivational

### Expanding Your Word Power
1. sweltering
2. oasis
3. tingle
4. prodigious
5. creed
6. hamlet
7. California
8. Pennsylvania

### Understanding Language
1. self-evident
2. slaveowners
3. mountainside
4. hilltops
5. snow-capped

### Expanding Other Skills
1. *I Have a Dream: The Life and Words of Martin Luther King, Jr.*
2. Martin Luther King Jr.
3. 1992
4. with the call number

## Page 66

### Expanding Your Reading Power
1. storytelling is popular
   storytelling could be a handy skill to develop
2. kids can become storytellers
3. Answers will vary.

### Expanding Your Word Power
1. solstice
2. placard
3. sentimental
4. reunion
5. gigs
6. enthusiasm
7. make time fly
8. to make time seem to pass quickly

### Understanding Language
1. b
2. c
3. d
4. a

### Expanding Other Skills
1. your own stories
   A. stories you enjoy
   B. stories that are appropriate for the audience
   C. your audience's reaction

## Page 68

### Expanding Your Reading Power
1. A, SA, SA, SA
2. O, O, F, O
3. 2, 1, 4, 3

### Expanding Your Word Power
1. adaptation
2. sympathetic
3. unison
4. rhythm
5. device
6. rousing
7. rest
8. watch

### Understanding Language
1. b
2. d
3. c
4. a

### Expanding Other Skills
the place of the performance
the date of the performance
the time of the performance
that it is a storytelling performance

## Page 70

### Expanding Your Reading Power
1. what Philo does
   what Philo says
   what Philo thinks
   how the author directly describes Philo
2. Answers will vary.
   a. He was curious.
   b. He tinkered with the generator.
   c. He read magazines.
3. Answers will vary.

### Expanding Your Word Power
| | | | |
|---|---|---|---|
| 1. wryly | | 2. fanfare |
| 3. awe | | 4. discarded |
| 5. generator | | 6. tinker |
| 7. mechanical, machine | | | |
| 8. band, orchestra | | | |

### Understanding Language
| | | | | | |
|---|---|---|---|---|---|
| 1. c | | 2. f | | 3. a |
| 4. b | | 5. e | | 6. d |

### Expanding Other Skills
1. habitation  2. metal  3. music

## Page 72

### Expanding Your Reading Power
1. Answers will vary.
2. contracted
3. concentration
4. from problem to solution

### Expanding Your Word Power
| | | |
|---|---|---|
| 1. harness | | 2. harrow |
| 3. tedious | | 4. patents |
5. transmission
6. He watched the stream of sunlight through the stained-glass window.

### Understanding Language
| | | |
|---|---|---|
| 1. c | | 2. b |
| 3. a | | 4. d |

### Expanding Other Skills
1. USA
2. Mali
3. Iraq, Mali, Samoa, South Africa

## Page 74

### Expanding Your Reading Power
1. 1, 4, 3, 2
2. imaginative, informative
3. T, T, F, T

### Expanding Your Word Power
| | | |
|---|---|---|
| 1. reluctantly | 2. nucleus |
| 3. atom | 4. vacuum |
| 5. molecules | 6. pixels |
| 7. accelerates | 8. contend |
| 9. horizontally | |

### Understanding Language
1. Philo's invention
2. atom's nucleus
3. colors' intensities

### Expanding Other Skills
| | |
|---|---|
| 1. stopped | stopping |
| 2. scanned | scanning |
| 3. synchronized | synchronizing |
| 4. varied | varying |

## Page 76

### Expanding Your Reading Power
1. BT, B, B, T
2. Similarities exist in how televisions and brains work.
3. The brain processes a lot of information. Stories are part of how the brain makes meaning.

### Expanding Your Word Power
| | | |
|---|---|---|
| 1. succession | 2. critical |
| 3. frequencies | 4. assuming |
| 5. perceived | 6. S |
| 7. M | 8. M |

### Understanding Language
1. newspaper  2. someone

### Expanding Other Skills
III. A. feels only the elephant's side
    B. says elephant is like a wall
IV. Third blind man
    A. feels only the elephant's ear
    B. says elephant is a fan
V. Fourth blind man
    A. feels only the elephant's leg
    B. says elephant is a tree

## Page 78

### Expanding Your Reading Power
1. to motivate readers to keep a journal
2. reread
3. inspiration

### Expanding Your Word Power
1. aspire
2. career
3. clarify
4. habit
5. The vase fell and broke into dozens of pieces.
6. Don't forget to record your progress as you go.

### Understanding Language
1. c
2. e
3. a
4. b
5. d

### Expanding Other Skills
B. Write frequently.
C. Write ideas down when they come.
D. Use writing to clarify goals and organize activities.
E. Use writing to help discover things about yourself.
F. Use a journal to help solve problems.
G. Use a journal to record good times.

## Page 80

### Expanding Your Reading Power
1. famous, encouraging
2. T, O, O, T
3. Answers will vary.

### Expanding Your Word Power
1. vigorously
2. proceed
3. displaced
4. gratifying
5. feasible
6. from the heart
7. sincerely

### Understanding Language
1. people's hands
2. writer's work
3. writers' works

### Expanding Other Skills
1. author, page number, date of magazine, article title, name of magazine
2. author, publisher, date of publication, book title, city of publication

## Page 82

### Expanding Your Reading Power
1. Answers will vary. Muses come from the myths of ancient Greece. They inspire artists. They help those who are actively working on a project, but will leave if they are ignored.
2. a. Be a careful observer.
   b. Work at your project.
   c. Keep a journal.
   d. Read daily.
   e. Use ideas when they come.
3. Answers will vary.

### Expanding Your Word Power
1. anticipating
2. tunic
3. frivolous
4. vicarious
5. genres
6. process
7. filmy, thin
8. gifts, sacrifices

### Understanding Language
1. c
2. d
3. e
4. a
5. b

### Expanding Other Skills
1. Answers will vary.

## Page 84

### Expanding Your Reading Power
1. We can have a variety of experiences through stories.
   Stories affect us more than we often realize.
   Ideas usually come when we follow a creative process.
2. 2, 4, 5, 3, 1
3. Answers will vary.

### Expanding Your Word Power
1. amiably
2. panicked
3. mused
4. crest
5. cast
6. wrote
7. stake
8. mean
9. cast

### Understanding Language
1. d
2. b
3. a
4. c

### Expanding Other Skills
1. a, e, f
2. e, f
3. c
4. a, b, f

# Notes

Five things I'm thankful for:

1. _____
2. _____
3. _____
4. _____
5. _____

# Notes

**Five things I'm thankful for:**

1. _____
2. _____
3. _____
4. _____
5. _____